The Bible Tells Us So

The Bible Tells Us So

R. B. KUIPER

The Banner of Truth Trust *78b Chiltern Street London* W1

FIRST PUBLISHED NOVEMBER 1968

Set in 10 *on* 12 *pt Plantin* 110
and printed and bound in England by
Hazell Watson & Viney Ltd
Aylesbury, Bucks

This final expression
of R. B. Kuiper's faith & love
is dedicated to his
children & grand-children,
whom he ever regarded
with an affectionate concern,
& who in turn
held him in loving esteem.
Marie J. Kuiper

Foreword

JOHN MURRAY

THE legacy of monographs from the pen of R. B. Kuiper is an abiding memorial to his Christian devotion and to the careful, well-balanced, informed thinking by which his preaching and writing were characterized. It is likely that *The Glorious Body of Christ* should be regarded as his masterpiece. But when the question of evangelism is so much in the forefront, it is to *God-Centred Evangelism* that the church does well to take heed. Here we have the theology of evangelism, and evangelism without scriptural theology has lost its moorings. The extent to which undiscriminating universalism has captivated the thought of the church creates dismay in those devoted to the whole counsel of God. *For Whom Did Christ Die?* deals with what is crucial in this issue.

The present volume occupies a unique place in R. B. Kuiper's legacy. This is so not because it is posthumous. It is unique for other reasons. It can almost be said that this work occupied his pen to his dying hour. This explains its unfinished character. As the final product of his pen the title sums up that to which R. B. Kuiper had given his life, to explore and apply the riches of God's Word. There was no antithesis in his mind between devotion to Scripture and devotion to the Lord. Any one who knew him or read his printed word became aware of the ardent love he bore to the Saviour and the jealousy he entertained for the Saviour's honour. But this jealousy was the measure of Kuiper's faith in the Bible as the inerrant, living, and abiding Word of God. Thus his epitaph: *The Bible Tells Us So.*

In the esteem of the present writer, there is another reason why these studies have a unique place in Kuiper's repertory. His writing, as his preaching and lecturing, was always characterized by clarity and simplicity. Obscurity of expression never marred his written or spoken word. This was the fruit of chastened scholarship, so much so that we are liable to overlook the mature thought behind it. Kuiper never made a display of erudition; such pretence he abhorred. But erudition of the truest hue there was, and the discerning could discover it in his penetrating and perspicuous analyses. These twelve brief chapters are fine examples of the qualities that adorned our beloved friend and colleague. I count it a privilege to have read them in typescript. The pleasure has been as great as the privilege and I look forward to the printed page for my own renewed benefit and that of countless other readers.

One would fain give many quotations from the pages that follow to illustrate the unsurpassed skill of simple expression, fine distinction, sound exposition, and humbling application. One will have to suffice. They are the concluding words of Chapter II: 'Let no one think that the divine law requires that we bestow most of our love on God and the remainder on our neighbour. It demands that we love God with our entire being, and that we love our neighbour for God's sake. And the minister who preaches for his own glory rather than God's glory is guilty of idolatry; but so is the minister who preaches for God's glory *and* his own.

'How it behoves each of God's children to smite his breast and pray, "God, be merciful to me, idolater that I am".'

Theologically, R. B. Kuiper was Reformed to the core of his being. He believed the Bible set forth one system of doctrine and this system was specifically Reformed. On this he knew no equivocation or compromise. For the maintenance and proclamation of the reformed faith he was supremely jealous and every deviation from it he fought to the end of his earthly pilgrimage. The devotion of his heart, voice, and pen continues to bear witness in this his final message to the church and to the world.

Bonar Bridge, Scotland JOHN MURRAY
29 *April* 1968

Preface

It is with a deep sense of gratitude to God for all that Professor R. B. Kuiper meant to me as gifted teacher, warm friend, reliable counsellor, superb preacher of the Word and loving father-in-law that I have prepared the following chapters for publication. Most of these chapters were in their original first-draft longhand form, although two of them had appeared as articles in Torch and Trumpet *and are reproduced here with some alterations and additions. Another chapter had been finished in typewritten form as a requested article.*

The author had his own style and I have carefully avoided doing anything to alter that. Dealing with a manuscript in its original draft raises special problems for the one whose task it is to render such writings in a form acceptable to a publisher. Any changes that have been made are the obvious ones that usually are called for in writings at such an early stage. I have known full well that Professor Kuiper had no patience with editors who took liberties with his work. It has been my intent to have Professor Kuiper speak in these pages in his own forceful, clear and inimitable manner. Whatever faults may be apparent in the finished product are to be ascribed, I am sure, to the undersigned and not to the author.

The Introduction *has been left as he left it, although it obviously is not complete. However, it has an adequate message as it is and certainly calls for nothing additional by another. It is also evident that the twelfth chapter is not complete. Here too the author's work was left as it came from his hand. The breaking off point is such that what goes before intimates pretty clearly what the author's line of thought was for the fully contemplated essay. The one regret is, of course, that we do not have the remaining chapters that this able and devoted churchman felt burdened to leave with the church on earth.*

Scriptural quotations are numerous in this work with its final appeal to the Word that R. B. loved to preach. It will be noted that the author has not always been consistent in his use of any one version of the Holy Bible. He used the text that he felt most aptly and correctly rendered God's Word and I have done nothing to seek consistency in the use of any one version. Most of the quotations are from the King James Version, although some are from the American Standard Version.

Whenever I ran into difficulty reading the manuscript in the author's handwriting I have had the benefit of competent help from his widow and his daughter Marietta, my wife. I am grateful for their assistance. And a special word of appreciation is due to Professor John Murray for his ready willingness to write a foreword to this volume. This ready willingness and the resulting product from Professor Murray's hand reflect the deep respect and esteem that marked the relationship between R. B. Kuiper and John Murray.

It is my sincere hope that this little volume from the mind and heart of a great preacher and a devoted servant of Jesus Christ may help some of Christ's own to grow in that faith to whose clear exposition and fervent proclamation Professor Kuiper gave the fine energies of his richly endowed life.

EDWARD HEEREMA

Bradenton, Florida

Contents

Foreword: *John Murray* 7

Preface: *Edward Heerema* 11

Introduction 15

I THE BIBLE IS GOD'S WORD 17
The reasons for accepting the Bible as the word of God . . . Subtle denials of the Bible as the word of God . . . The importance of upholding the Bible as the word of God

II GOD IS 26
The existence of God . . . Atheism . . . Idolatry

III GOD IS SOVEREIGN 35
Divine sovereignty defined . . . Divine sovereignty and His foreordination . . . Divine sovereignty and predestination . . . The sovereignty of God and His commandments

IV MAN IS A RESPONSIBLE BEING 43
The basis of human responsibility . . . Man's responsibility and his eternal destiny

V GOD IS ALMIGHTY 51
The boundless power of God . . . Omnipotence and the will of God . . . Omnipotence and salvation . . . Divine omnipotence denied . . . Proper contemplation of the divine omnipotence

VI THE LOVE OF GOD IS INFINITE 61
Love transcending universalism . . . Love embracing all living men . . . Love differentiating between men

VII SALVATION BELONGS TO THE TRIUNE GOD 71

God the Father saves . . . God the Son saves . . . God the Holy Spirit saves

VIII SALVATION IS BY GRACE ALONE 81

The doctrine in Scripture . . . The doctrine in history . . . The doctrine in particular . . . The doctrine in practice

IX SALVATION IS BY FAITH ALONE 92

The distinctiveness of saving faith . . . Some prerequisites of saving faith . . . The essence of saving faith . . . The proof of saving faith

X CHRISTIANITY IS THE ONE TRUE RELIGION 102

The only true Word . . . The only true God . . . The only true Saviour . . . The only true morality

XI THE ANTITHESIS OF THE REGENERATE AND THE UNREGENERATE IS RADICAL 113

Central in Scripture, not peripheral . . . A fact, not a duty . . . Spiritual, not spatial . . . Absolute, not relative . . . Pervasive, not partial . . . Active, not passive . . . Issuing in conquest, not flight

XII CHRISTIANITY IS HISTORY, DOCTRINE, CONDUCT 128

Christianity is history . . . Christianity is doctrine

Introduction

THE following essays, containing many excerpts from sermons that I have preached, are meant to be popular presentations of basic teachings of the Christian religion over against current distortions and denials. Obviously, I have had to be selective. What basic Christian doctrine is not under fire today? It has been my aim to uphold such doctrines as at once are most basic and are most vigorously attacked. And in making my choices I have had in mind the interests and needs of the man in the pew not less than those of the professional theologian.

As the title of this volume indicates, the presupposition underlying this entire volume is that the Bible is the infallible and inerrant Word of God. For that reason my appeal throughout is not to the speculations of philosophers, or for that matter of theologians, but to Holy Scripture. Yet, by giving due consideration to the interpretation of Scripture by others I have sought to avoid the folly of relying unduly on my own interpretation.

It has often been said that in order to be a good theologian one must be a good exegete. That is very true. No one has the right to force his theology on Scripture. Contrariwise, everybody must derive his theology from Scripture. But it is just as true that in order to be a good exegete of Scripture one must be a good theologian. The Bible is a self-consistent unit. What it teaches in one place it does not contradict elsewhere. Scriptural paradoxes are seeming, not actual, contradictions. Scripture is its own infallible interpreter. And every part of it must be interpreted in the light of the whole of it.

God's children know only in part. They do not have nearly all the answers. Yet to a great many important questions God has given unmistakable answers in his Word. Under the illumination of the Holy Spirit, the Christian church, having the promise of the Spirit of truth [*John* 14:17], has distilled what Scripture calls 'the faith once for all delivered to the saints'. For that faith the saints are in sacred duty bound to 'contend earnestly' [*Jude* 3]. This little volume is an attempt to do just that.

Today few things are being impressed upon the minds of men so emphatically as that they are living in a world of change. How true that is! However, for that very reason men need greatly to be reminded of the eternal truths of the Word of God. And they need to be told that the unchangeable is of incomparably greater importance than is that which is subject to change.

R.B.K.

I
The Bible is God's Word

CERTAIN teachings are of the essence of Christianity. Often they are spoken of as Christian fundamentals. They are indeed basic to the Christian religion. The doctrine that the Bible is the Word of God is the most basic of them all, for the whole of Christianity is derived from the Bible. All Christian teachings, whether doctrinal or ethical, are drawn from the Bible. According to Christianity the acid test of truth and goodness is Scripturalness.

THE REASONS FOR ACCEPTING THE BIBLE AS THE WORD OF GOD

There are so-called rational arguments for the proposition that the Bible is the Word of God. Following are some of them.

The Bible contains prophecies which have been strikingly fulfilled. For a few examples, the Old Testament foretold that the Saviour would be born in Bethlehem [*Mic* 5:2], that his mother would be a virgin [*Isa* 7:14], that men would cast lots over his clothing [*Ps* 22:18]. The New Testament tells us that all this came to pass. Obviously only God, who sees the things of tomorrow as if they had happened yesterday, can predict future events in such detail and with such precision. That is an excellent argument.

The sixty-six books of the Bible were written by a considerable number of men – we do not know exactly how many – over some sixteen centuries. Yet the Bible never contradicts itself. That is a remarkable fact. Two books on related subjects written sixteen years apart by one man would almost certainly contain a number of inconsistencies. The self-consistency of the Bible is evidence that its human authors were all of them controlled by one mind, the mind of the Holy Spirit. Those to the contrary notwithstanding who contend that the Bible contains contradictions, that too is an excellent argument.

Throughout the centuries the Bible has been attacked as no other book ever was, but it has withstood every onslaught. For example, the critics used to say that Moses could not possibly have written the first five books of the Bible, the Pentateuch, for the simple reason that writing was unknown in his day. By this time we know that already in the days of Abraham the Canaanites corresponded with one another by means of inscribed tablets. That fact coupled with the fact that Moses was 'instructed in all the wisdom of the Egyptians' [*Acts* 7:22] utterly destroys this contention. For one more example, the Old Testament makes frequent mention of 'the Hittites'. It has been asserted that no such people existed. But inscriptions discovered some years ago in the Orient speak of the Hittites as an influential nation. Again the critics were wrong, the Bible was right. Instances of that kind could easily be multiplied. The story of the blacksmith who piled up in a corner of his shop all the hammers which had been broken over several decades on one anvil, while, of course, proving nothing, can illustrate rather aptly the point at issue. The Bible resembles that anvil; the attacks made on the Bible are like those broken hammers. One is reminded of the words of wisdom spoken by Gamaliel to the Jewish Sanhedrin with reference to the preaching of the apostles: 'If this counsel or this work be of men, it will be overthrown: but if it is of God, ye will not be able to overthrow them; lest haply ye be found even to be fighting against God' [*Acts* 5:38, 39].

The Bible's influence, too is an argument for its being the Word of God. It has been instrumental in transforming the most wicked of men into saints, criminals into Christians. It is beyond all doubt the most powerful means by which God operates among and in the children of men. It is 'living and active, and sharper than any two-edged sword, and piercing even to the dividing of soul and spirit, of both joints and marrow, and quick to discern the thoughts and intents of the heart' [*Heb* 4:12].

Let us suppose that the foregoing arguments, and several others just as forceful as these, are presented to an infidel. Let us further suppose that the infidel is silenced by those arguments. Does it follow that he has become a believer? Not necessarily. God may, perhaps, use such argumentation as a means to lead the unbeliever to faith, but it takes more than mere argumentation to transform him into a believer. Popularly put, unbelief is a matter not only of the head, but of the heart. The unbeliever's trouble is that his heart is not right with God. And only God the Holy Spirit is able to give a heart of flesh for one of stone. That he does in bestowing the grace of regeneration, the new birth.

There are compelling reasons for accepting the Bible as the Word of God in what theologians speak of as 'the testimony of the Holy Spirit'. That testimony is twofold. The Holy Spirit testifies in the heart of the regenerated person that the Bible is the Word of God. That is commonly called his internal testimony. The Holy Spirit also testifies in the Bible itself that the Bible is the Word of God. That is usually designated his external testimony.

To elucidate what is meant by the inward testimony of the Holy Spirit an illustration may prove helpful. Mr Smith and

Mr Jones are seated in the same room. From behind a closed door comes a voice. Smith queries, 'Who is that speaking?' Jones replies, 'It's my father.' Smith asks, 'How do you know it is your father?' Jones answers, 'Of course, it is my father. Don't I know my own father? And if I know him wouldn't I recognize his voice?' Who has been born again knows God. Not only does he have some, or for that matter, much, knowledge about God; he knows God in the sense in which Jesus used that term when he said: 'This is life eternal, that they should know thee, the only true God, and him whom thou didst send, even Jesus Christ' [*John* 17:3]. Because he knows God he recognizes the voice of God coming to him in Holy Writ.

That the Holy Spirit witnesses in the Bible to the Bible's being the Word of God is clear from such passages as II *Timothy* 3:16 – 'All scripture is given by inspiration of God, and is profitable for doctrine, for reproof, for correction, for instruction in righteousness' and II *Peter* 1:21 – 'No prophecy ever came by the will of man, but men spake from God, being moved by the Holy Spirit.'

Incidentally it may be said here that the authoritative Scriptures are, of course, the original manuscripts. Their authors were led by the Holy Spirit so as to record the Word of God infallibly. And, although subsequent copyists were not so led, it is evident that throughout the centuries God has kept watch over the text of the Bible with a very special providence. As Edward J. Young has said so well in *Thy Word is Truth*: 'In His mysterious providence, God has preserved His Word. We do not have a Bible which is unreliable and glutted with error, but one that in most wondrous fashion presents the Word of God and the text of the original' (p. 61).

SUBTLE DENIALS OF THE BIBLE AS THE WORD OF GOD

Scripture tells us that Satan goes about as a roaring lion seeking whom he may devour [I *Pet* 5:8]. It also tells us that the father of lies often operates deceptively as an angel of light [II *Cor* 11:14]. He and his servants have made, and are making, some truly subtle attacks on the Bible as the Word of God.

There are at least two ways of destroying a house. The obvious and quick way is to blow it up with dynamite. A less obvious and slower, but in the long run no less effective way, is to break it down one brick or one board at a time. Admittedly the latter way has an advantage over the former. It will not shock the sensibilities of the occupants of the house quite so much. In his striving to destroy the foundation of the faith of God's saints, namely God's excellent Word, the great deceiver often employs subtle devices.

The Roman Catholic Church has always confessed the Bible to be the infallible Word of God. In these days of rapprochement of Roman Catholicism and Protestantism that fact is receiving much emphasis. However, Rome has always denied, and still keeps denying, the sufficiency of the Bible as the Word of God. It teaches that there are two infallibles: the Bible and the Church. And so it holds tenaciously to certain teachings which, although not found in the Bible, have the backing of tradition. Among them are the doctrine of purgatory, the doctrine of the immaculate conception of the Virgin Mary by her mother Anna, and, since November 1, 1950, the doctrine of the assumption of Mary into heaven. Protestant Mystics are guilty of a similar error. They too say that special revelation was not completed when the sixty-six books of the Bible had been written. Special revelation, say they, is continuous. It comes to them, they claim, through the 'inner light', the 'Christian consciousness', and 'religious experience'. So corrupt is human nature that he who today places something else on a par with the Bible is practically certain to exalt that other thing above the Bible tomorrow. And so it is not strange that many traditions of the Roman Catholic Church contradict the Bible. Nor is it surprising that mysticism, prevalent as it is among liberal Protestants, sets much more store by subjective religious experience than by the objective Word of God.

One of the most ancient of all heresies is that the Word of God is in the Bible but the Bible is not the Word of God. That heresy is also extremely prevalent today. It has been said that only the New Testament is the Word of God, not the Old; that only the words of Jesus in the New Testament are the Word of God, not the words, for example, of Paul; that of the words of Jesus only the Sermon on the Mount is the Word of God. Karl Barth, who has long told us that the Bible *becomes* the Word of God when it truly affects the reader or hearer, also assures us that the Bible *is* the Word of God although it contains numerous human errors. Emil Brunner has said that listening to the Bible is much like listening to a phonograph record of Caruso. As in the latter case one hears the voice of the great Italian tenor but also at least a little scratching of the needle on the record, even in the case of Hi-Fi, so in the former case one hears the voice of the infallible God but also unavoidably the voices of the fallible human authors of the Bible. A young preacher once told me that he could put the stamp of his approval on the teaching of the Lord Jesus by and large, the only exception being Jesus' teaching of eternal punishment. What is truly alarming and highly deceptive, some self-styled conservative theologians are agreeing with the Socinians, the liberals of the Reformation age, that the Bible is indeed the infallible rule for faith and life, but contains many teachings which have no direct bearing on faith and life and in those teachings is fallible.

To name one more deceptive denial of the Bible as the Word of God, there are those who say that the authority of the Bible is only that of an expert. As the ancient Greeks were expert in matters of art and the ancient Romans were expert in matters of law, so, we are told, the ancient Hebrews were expert in matters of religion; and the Bible came into being when the most expert of these Hebrew experts recorded their religious experiences. We are advised that it would be foolish of us to refuse to give heed to those experts. However, even experts are fallible. Before the great depression of the thirties more than one expert financier kept predicting uninterrupted prosperity. And expert astronomers are not agreed on the composition of the moon. If the Bible has only the authority of an expert, it is fallible. But the Bible claims to come with the authority of the sovereign God. 'Thus saith the Lord' is its theme. In short, it lays claim to divine infallibility.

THE IMPORTANCE OF UPHOLDING THE BIBLE AS THE WORD OF GOD

There is a story of an army which had suffered defeat in battle and was now in precipitate flight. The victorious army kept shooting down one fleeing soldier after another. However, at long last the defeated army arrived at a place of safe retreat, the only thing wrong with it by then being that not a single soldier was left alive. That story has been applied to the Bible. Once we grant that not the entire Bible is the Word of God, we are sure to lose one part after another until finally nothing is left of it but the covers. So we are told. Is that an exaggeration? Rather it is an understatement. He who would decide by his own wisdom what in the Bible is the Word of God and what is not, is not *going to lose* the entire Bible but *has lost* it. By the very act of setting himself up as the judge of the Bible he has denied that it is the Word of the sovereign God.

Many theologians today tell us that the Bible is not the infallible Word of God but a fallible human witness to the infallible personal Word of God, Jesus Christ. Confusion worse confounded is difficult to imagine. How do we know that Jesus is the infallible personal Word of God but from the Bible? If the Bible is fallible, perhaps this teaching of the Bible is in error. And did not Jesus himself tell us that the Bible is infallible? He asserted, 'The Scripture cannot be broken' – and affirmed, 'Thy Word is truth' [*John* 10:35, 17:17]. He declared, 'Think not that I am come to destroy the law or the prophets: I am not come to destroy, but to fulfil. For verily I say unto you, Till heaven and earth pass, one jot or one tittle shall in no wise pass from the law, till all be fulfilled' [*Matt* 5:17–18]. If the written Word is not infallible, the personal Word is a liar. In short, nothing could be clearer than that the infallibility of the Bible and the infallibility of the Christ stand or fall together. He who denies the former rejects the latter.

Two supremely important questions are with us every moment of our lives. It is utterly impossible to dodge either of them. They are: *What is true?* and *What is good?* God has answered both of these questions for us in the Bible, and, of course, his answers are right. To reject the Bible as the Word of God is to reject those answers. And he who does that is like a vessel drifting on the ocean without rudder or compass. He is *at sea* in the most complete and most terrifying sense of that term.

He who rejects the Bible as the Word of God has nothing to *live* by. Neither does he have anything to *die* by. Unless we are going to live until the second coming of our Lord, all of us are sure to die. 'It is appointed unto men once to die, but after this the judgment' [*Heb* 9:27]. Are we ready for the judgment? Are we prepared to meet God? We are only if we believe in him whose name is the only name 'under heaven given among men whereby we must be saved' [*Acts* 4:12] and who declared, 'I am the way, the truth, and the life; no man cometh unto the Father but by me' [*John* 14:6]. The one and only Saviour is *the Christ of Holy Scripture.*

II

God is

WHEN from the bush which burned but was not consumed God called Moses to lead Israel out of Egypt's iron furnace, Moses asked what he would have to say if the children of Israel should inquire after the name of the God who had sent him. The divine answer was, 'I AM THAT I AM' [*Ex* 3:14]. The context shows that God's direct reference in so naming himself was to his unchanging faithfulness to his covenant people. The God of Abraham, Isaac and Jacob was also the God of their descendants and would deliver them from bondage. However, underlying this self-revelation of God was the fact of his being. He exists in an entirely unique sense, as none of his creatures does. He is the self-existent and unchangeable One. He is 'the first and the last' [*Isa* 41:4, 44:6, 48:12]. He is pure Being. He alone truly *is*.

This is not to say that philosopher Paul Tillich was right when he defined God as 'the ground of all being'. That definition has pantheistic implications. But the Bible teaches the very opposite of Pantheism. Instead of identifying God and the universe it indicates that God is altogether different from his creatures. Creation had a beginning, and it owes its beginning as well as its continuance to God. God exists independently. He alone is 'from everlasting to everlasting' [*Ps* 90:2].

THE EXISTENCE OF GOD

There are so-called rational or philosophical proofs for the existence of God. To name some of them, there is the ontological argument, which deduces the existence of God from the fact that man has an idea of God; the cosmological argument, which says that the material universe must have God as its adequate cause; the teleological argument, which insists that the order and purpose evident in the universe demand an intelligent cause adequate for its production; and the moral argument, which tells us that man's quest for a moral ideal necessitates the existence of a God who imparts reality to that ideal.

There is much difference of opinion among philosophers, and among theologians too, as to the validity of these arguments. We are not now concerned to evaluate them. Our one concern is to state what the Bible teaches about the existence of God.

The Bible does not argue for the existence of God; it takes this existence for granted. The very first verse of the Bible does that. Preachers often present that verse as if there were a period after 'God'. And then they proceed to tell their audiences that the first teaching of the Bible is that God exists. Such is not the case. The first verse of the Bible does not tell us that God exists, but what God, whose existence is presupposed, did in the beginning. He created heaven and earth.

Theologians distinguish between God's general revelation in nature and in history and his special revelation in the Bible. The distinction is valid. And it is correct to say that the former does not teach us how we may be saved from sin and spiritual death and hell, while the latter teaches us all we need to know on that important subject. However, let no one think that these two revelations at any point contradict each other. Contrariwise they are in perfect harmony. Nor does the latter exclude the former. The Bible tells us a great deal about general revelation. One deeply important truth it teaches is that God created the universe. It also tells us that general revelation gives conclusive evidence of the existence of God. Says the psalmist, 'The heavens declare the glory of God, and the firmament showeth his handiwork' [*Ps* 19:1]. And the apostle Paul describes even the heathen as in a sense 'knowing God' because 'the invisible things of him since the creation of the world are clearly seen, being perceived through the things that are made, even his everlasting power and divinity' [*Rom* 1:20, 21].

Nature, in which God reveals himself, includes the nature of man. The Bible tells us that man was made in the image of God [*Gen* 1:27]. That image makes man *man*. The Bible also tells us that, although this image was seriously marred and even largely lost through sin, yet vestiges of it remain in fallen man. He has become neither a devil nor a brute beast. He remains a human being. In consequence he has a 'sense of the divine'. That great church father Augustine of Hippo, was right when he said that man, having been created for God, cannot rest until he finds rest in God. In consequence fallen men, totally depraved though they are and utterly incapable of finding God, may be said to be groping after God. Calvin said, 'Though no corner of the world be void of the testimony of God's glory, yet we need not go without ourselves to lay hold upon Him. For He doth affect and move every one of us inwardly with His power in such sort that . . . in feeling Him we feel Him not. In this respect certain of the philosophers called man a microcosm (little world), because he is above all other creatures a token of God's glory' [Commentary on *Acts* 17:27].

In short, man has a religious nature. Man has been said to be 'incurably religious'. But that expression is not a happy one, for it presupposes that religion is a disease. It is far better to say that man is *constitutionally* religious. That accounts for the fact that even the most uncivilized tribe of people has some sort of religion. It also accounts for the fact that no man is a consistent atheist. During the second World War it was often said that there were no atheists in fox-holes. How true! To the point is the story of the infidel who boldly denied the existence of God and his own immortal soul, but when condemned to the gallows because of murder, prayed just before the trap was sprung, 'O God, if there be a God, save my soul, if I have a soul'.

Small wonder that the Bible calls him that denies the existence of God a 'fool' [*Ps* 14:1, 53:1]. He denies what God says in the Bible. He denies what all nature and all history proclaim. He denies what his own nature tells him. He denies what he knows to be true. The very vehemence with which he denies God is evidence of his hypocrisy.

ATHEISM

Atheism is rampant today. Much of it is vocal, but not all of it.

There are those who blatantly deny the existence of God, much as did Robert G. Ingersoll when he challenged God, if indeed God existed, to strike him down dead. Of late certain self-styled 'Christian' theologians are telling us that God is 'dead'. Let it be said emphatically that they are receiving far more attention than they deserve. The Bible makes short shrift of them. It characterizes them as 'fools' [*Ps* 14:1]. Also, the most basic tenet of Communism is atheism.

There are also those – agnostics by name – who, affirming that man does not know and indeed cannot know whether there is a God, ignore him. Many there are who, without giving any serious thought to the question whether or not God exists, order their lives in practice as if he does not. It is not unusual for men who confess to believe in God to call on him only in times of deep distress after the manner of the familiar rhyme:

God and the doctor we both adore
In time of trouble, not before.
The illness cured, reverses righted,
God is forgotten, the doctor slighted.

One of the greatest and most prevalent evils of our day is secularism. It consists of the divorcing of either some or all of human life from God.

On the American scene secularism comes to forceful expression in a grave misinterpretation of the First Amendment to the Constitution of the United States. It reads in part: 'Congress shall make no law respecting an establishment of religion, or prohibiting the free exercise thereof.' Obviously that amendment rules out for these United States an established or state church, such as many European countries had at the time of its adoption and some still have today. The Church of England and the Hervormde Kerk of the Netherlands are examples. In short, this amendment requires what is loosely denominated the separation of state and church. But today many insist that it demands the separation of the state from all religion. That no such thing was the intent of the founding fathers is clear from such simple facts as that the sessions of Congress are customarily opened with prayer, that the President of the United States on assuming office is required to take an oath, that the federal government has long provided chaplains for our armed forces, and that to this day the American people on many of their coins profess 'In God we trust'. In fact, the First Amendment itself upholds for all Americans freedom of religion and plainly implies that it is a duty of the state to protect that freedom. The separation of the state and religion is outright secularism. It is also one of the greatest fallacies of twentieth-century Americans.

Due in large part to that fallacy the public schools in these United States have been almost completely secularized. Time was when these schools by and large were Christian or at least honoured the Christian tradition. Gradually, however, in fact sometimes rapidly, religious neutrality so-called took over. In many instances under the guise of neutrality anti-Christian teachings prevailed. In recent years the United States Supreme Court has accelerated and in fact practically completed the process of de-Christianization.

At this point American Christians confront a serious dilemma. On the one hand, they will have to grant as most of them do that education must be religious. Education divorced from religion is unworthy of its name. Religion must permeate education. On the other hand, the opinion prevails in this nation that the state is in duty bound to observe religious neutrality. Does it not follow as the night the day that such a state must get out of the business of educating? To a great many that conclusion will no doubt seem extremely radical, but obviously it is unavoidable. Nor should it surprise Christians, for the Word of God assigns the task of education not to the state, but to the family. Parents, not rulers, are to 'train up a child in the way he should go' [*Prov* 22:6].

Problems remain. As the last word has not been said on the relation of church and state to each other, so the final word has not been said on the relation of the state to religion. For instance, should all Christians press, as do those Reformed Presbyterians who are known as Covenanters, for the inclusion in the United States Constitution of the name of Christ as Head of this nation, or should the church of Christ rest content when moral and religious issues face the nation to demand of the state that it heed the Word of God?

Let not the readers view the foregoing reflections on secularism as a diversion. We were on the subject of atheism and we still are. Secularism is atheism. The isolation of the whole of one's life from God is radical secularism and obviously is atheism. The isolation of part of one's life from God is less radical secularism but still atheism. For God is a totalitarian Ruler who demands full allegiance from his subjects. Of him, through him, and unto him are all things; therefore all things must be unto him [*Rom* 11:36]. Every one of his subjects must do to God's glory his eating, his drinking, and whatever he does [1 *Cor* 10:31]. To withhold from him any part of one's life is to deny that he is truly God.

IDOLATRY

Because man is constitutionally religious, he who denies God's existence cannot possibly avoid idolatry. Whether or not he admits this, he who rejects the true God is bound to substitute a false God for Him.

There are idols innumerable. Fetishes, images of man or beast, heavenly bodies, souls of departed ancestors, the state, money, pleasure, science – all these and many others are worshipped by men. But all idols have one thing in common. All of them alike are creatures. All idolaters worship 'the creature rather than the Creator' [*Rom* 1:25].

There are men who avowedly worship Satan. In fact all idolatry pleases Satan and his angels, the one devil and his numerous demons. No wonder Moses charged idolatrous Israel with sacrificing unto demons [*Deut* 32:17].

Ever since man ruined the image of God in which he had been created he has been fashioning gods in his own image. That is to say, all idols are the product of human imagination. Rejecting God's revelation of himself, men have been telling

God what he ought to be like. In so doing man sets himself up as God. And so the great question from the fall of man to the present day has been and is: Who is God? *Is God God or is man God?*

Idolatry can be reduced still further to a common denominator. Ultimately all idolatry amounts to the worship by the idolater of himself, what is popularly known as 'big I'. When the first man broke God's commandment he rejected God as God and in effect declared himself to be God. Such is the essence of all sin. It is rebellion against God and deification of self. Not infrequently such rebellion and such deification become vocal. There are those who say, 'I cannot believe in a triune God, for the doctrine of the trinity does not make sense to my intellect'. There are those who say, 'A God who demands a bloody sacrifice for sin, notably the bloody sacrifice of his own Son, is in my estimation "nothing but a dirty bully", for I would not think of making such a demand.' There are those who say, 'It cannot be true that God sentences men to eternal hell, for I could not possibly bring myself to do such a thing.' There are those who say, 'It is inconceivable that God decreed from eternity the damnation of some of his creatures, for such a decree would be unworthy of me.' In each of these instances there is a rejection of the God of the Bible and the substitution for him of self. That is to say, each is an instance of idolatry.

Significantly, the very first commandment of the divine law for man is, 'Thou shalt have no other gods before me' [*Ex* 20:3, *Deut* 5:7]. In its interpretation of that commandment the Heidelberg Catechism defines idolatry not only as placing one's trust in any other object *instead of* the one true God who has revealed himself in his Word, but also as placing one's trust in another object *besides* that God. He who trusts in his goodness or his church *instead of* God to save his soul is an idolater. So is he who trusts for salvation in God *and* his own goodness or his church. And so is he who trusts God to take care of him for the life hereafter, but trusts in his own money or wisdom or morality to take him through this life.

One positive demand of the first commandment is that we love God with our whole heart, our whole soul, all our mind and all our strength [*Deut.* 6:5, *Matt* 22:37, *Mark* 12:30, *Luke* 10:27]. He who withholds his love from God and bestows it on another is an idolater. So is he who divides his love between God and another. Let no one think that the divine law requires that we bestow most of our love on God and the remainder on our neighbour. It demands that we love God with our entire being, and that we love our neighbour for God's sake. And the minister who preaches for his own glory rather than God's glory is guilty of idolatry; but so is the minister who preaches for God's glory *and* his own.

How it behoves each of God's children to smite his breast and pray, 'God, be merciful to me, idolater that I am.'

III

God is sovereign

THE word *sovereign* is derived from the Latin *supremus*, which means *highest*. Incidentally, from a philological viewpoint the spelling *soveren* is to be preferred, the spelling *sovereign* having resulted from confusion with the word *reign*. The Dutch spelling *souverein* and the French spelling *souvrain* are quite correct. Only because the spelling *sovereign* has become prevalent will it be employed in this chapter.

DIVINE SOVEREIGNTY DEFINED

What is the sovereignty of God?

Perhaps it should be said at the very outset that divine sovereignty is not arbitrariness. God is not, as some have thought, an oriental despot who is guided by his every whim. God has no whims. Contrariwise, God does all that he does because he is who he is, and his own all-embracing attribute is perfection. 'God is love' [1 *John* 4:8]. He is 'just and true' in all his ways [*Rev* 15:3]. The seraphs cry one to another, 'Holy holy, holy is the Lord of hosts' [*Isa* 6:3].

What then is the divine sovereignty? Even pagan Nebuchadnezzar admitted, 'He doeth according to his will in the army of heaven, and among the inhabitants of the earth; and none can stay his hand or say unto him, What doest thou?' [*Dan* 4:35]. Isaiah put the rhetorical question, 'Who hath directed the

Spirit of the Lord, or being his counsellor hath taught him? With whom took he counsel, and who instructed him, and taught him in the path of judgment, and taught him knowledge, and showed to him the way of understanding?' [*Isa* 40:13, 14]. The apostle Paul exclaimed, 'O the depth of the riches both of the wisdom and knowledge of God! How unsearchable are his judgments and his ways past finding out! For who hath known the mind of the Lord? or who hath been his counsellor? Or who hath first given to him, and it shall be recompensed unto him again? For of him, and through him, and unto him, are all things; to whom be glory for ever. Amen' [*Rom* 11:33–36]. The sovereignty of God may be defined as his absolute right to govern and dispose of all his creatures according to his good pleasure. And, not to be forgotten, God not only *has* that right; he *exercises* it.

The term *sovereignty* is often used in a relative sense. For example, Calvinists often speak of 'sphere sovereignty'. What they mean is that the individual, the family, the state and the church are sovereign each in its own sphere, and not beyond that sphere. In these days of rising state totalitarianism that needs to be emphasized. The individual, the family and the church have certain rights, bestowed upon them by God, on which the state has no right to impinge. And the Roman Catholic Church may well be reminded that the individual, the family and the state have certain rights, bestowed upon them by God, with which the church has no right to interfere. The sovereignty of God, however, is boundless and absolute. He is sovereign over the individual, the family, the state and the church – over all his creatures, over the whole of the universe. His rule is truly totalitarian.

Hence it must be said that God alone is sovereign. To revert to the etymology or derivation of the term, *sovereign* means *highest*. Obviously, there can be but one who is highest. Let me illustrate. A village has three churches. Each church has a steeple, and all three steeples are of precisely the same height. Which is highest? The very question is, of course, absurd. There can never be more than one highest. If God is truly sovereign, sovereignty belongs to him *alone*. The Bible tells us most emphatically that precisely this is the case.

DIVINE SOVEREIGNTY AND HIS FOREORDINATION

The sovereignty of God comes to expression in his decree of foreordination. The Westminster Shorter Catechism defines that decree as 'his eternal purpose, according to the counsel of his will, whereby, for his own glory, he hath foreordained whatsoever comes to pass'. Paul had it in mind when he asserted that God 'worketh all things after the counsel of his will' [*Eph* 1:11].

God's decree is *unalterable*. Being immutable, God never changes his mind. To deny the immutability of God is to deny that he is God. When the Bible states that God repents of this or that, it is employing a figure of speech, anthropomorphism, just as it employs this figure of speech when it ascribes to God parts of the human body. God declares, 'My counsel shall stand, and I will do all my pleasure' [*Isa* 46:10].

God's decree is *unconditional*. To be sure, the various elements in the decree are mutually dependent. In other words, the decree embraces not only *ends* but also *means* to ends. For instance, God decreed not only that a farmer would harvest 10,800 bushels of wheat in a given season, but also that he would plough, harrow, sow, etc. in order to obtain the harvest. Likewise, God decreed not only that my child would recover from serious illness, but that it would recover in answer to my prayers. However, no particular in the decree is dependent on anything not decreed. The obvious reason is that the decree includes *all* that comes to pass. Nothing not decreed ever happens.

God's decree is *all-comprehensive.* It includes all that comes to pass, sin included. In his Pentecostal sermon Peter said to the Jews concerning Jesus of Nazareth, 'Him, being delivered by the determinate counsel and foreknowledge of God, ye have taken, and by wicked hands have crucified and slain' [*Acts* 2:23]. Addressing God in prayer, the disciples at Jerusalem said, 'Of a truth against thy holy child Jesus, whom thou hast anointed, both Herod and Pontius Pilate, with the Gentiles and the people of Israel, were gathered together, for to do whatsoever thy hand and thy counsel determined before to be done' [*Acts* 4:27–28]. Significantly the Lamb of God is said to have been 'slain from the foundation of the world' [*Rev* 13:8]. From eternity God planned both sin and redemption.

God's decree is *efficacious.* This does not mean that God brings to pass by the direct application of his will and his power all things included in his decree. God did not force Adam and Eve to eat of the forbidden tree, nor did he compel Judas to betray Jesus. To say that he did is to make God the author of sin, which he most certainly and emphatically is not. It does mean that all that God has decreed will under the control of his providence certainly come to pass and that nothing can thwart this purpose. 'The counsel of the Lord standeth forever, the thoughts of his heart to all generations' [*Ps* 33:11].

DIVINE SOVEREIGNTY AND PREDESTINATION

If God foreordained from eternity *all* that would come to pass, he must have foreordained also the eternal destiny of men. The Bible teaches unmistakably that he did just that. The doctrine of sovereign predestination looms exceedingly large on the pages of Holy Writ. Paul taught that whom God did foreknow, that is, whom he loved from all eternity, them he also predestinated, called, justified and glorified [*Rom* 8:29–30]; and he told the saints at Ephesus that God chose them in Christ before the foundation of the world that they should be holy and without blame before him, in love having predestinated them unto the adoption of children by Jesus Christ, according to the good pleasure of his will [*Eph* 1:4, 5]. It must be noted that Paul did not say that God's choice was determined by the worthiness of the object of his choice, for instance, by their foreseen faith and obedience. He asserted that God chose 'according to the good pleasure of his will', that is, sovereignly. He also asserted that God did his choosing 'in love', for it is altogether likely that the phrase 'in love' at the conclusion of the fourth verse modifies the participle 'having predestinated' at the beginning of the fifth. In short, we are told that in choosing unto eternal life certain persons out of the fallen human race God is motivated by sovereign love.

The scriptural doctrine of election is unpopular. Even more unpopular is its so-called corollary, the doctrine of preterition or reprobation. Universalists, who are by no means confined to the Unitarian Universalist Church, tell us that a God of love cannot possibly have predestinated some of his rational creatures to eternal suffering. Karl Barth teaches that there are not two groups of human beings, the one elected to eternal life and the other foreordained to eternal reprobation, but that Christ is elect for all men and also reprobate for all. How he can escape the heresy of universal salvation is indeed puzzling. Strange to say, a growing number of supposedly Reformed theologians, perhaps under the influence of Barth, are questioning the scripturalness of this doctrine, and suggesting that it is a mere deduction by faulty human reason from the doctrine of election.

And yet, the doctrine is undeniably taught in Holy Writ. Jesus said, 'Many are called, but few are chosen' [*Matt* 22:14].

That the number of those who are chosen is small in comparison with the number of those who are called is part and parcel of the biblical doctrine of election. Inspired Paul made a sharp distinction between 'the vessels of wrath fitted to destruction' and 'the vessels of mercy, which he had afore prepared unto glory' [*Rom* 9:22, 23]. Inspired Peter spoke of 'them which stumble at the word, being disobedient; whereunto also they were appointed' [I *Pet* 2:8]. The very verb employed in the New Testament to designate election means to choose out of a larger number. That not all are chosen is not a deduction from election but inherent in it.

Small wonder that the Canons of Dort deal with preterition or reprobation not as a deduction from election but as an integral phase of it. They say, 'What peculiarly tends to illustrate and recommend to us the eternal and unmerited grace of election is the express testimony of sacred Scripture that not all, but some only, are elected, while others are passed by in the eternal decree ...' [I, 15].

Herman Bavinck, that most painstakingly Reformed theologian, taught that although God is not pleased with the damnation of the reprobate as he is pleased with the salvation of the elect, yet predestination is twofold. He insisted that faith is not the cause of election nor is sin the cause of preterition, but both are rooted solely in the sovereign good pleasure of God. And he distinguished between preterition and reprobation. God sovereignly passed by certain persons in the counsel of election. That was preterition. God decreed to punish these persons for their sins with eternal damnation. That is reprobation [*Gereformeerde Dogmatiek*, II, 397–425].

The conclusion is inevitable that one cannot reject the doctrine of reprobation without doing serious violence to the scriptural doctrine of election. It is equally clear that he who rejects the doctrine of reprobation faces a formidable dilemma:

either he must accept the heresy of universal salvation or he must deny that God foreordained from eternity *all* that comes to pass, which denial involves the rejection of the absolute sovereignty of God.

Note must be taken of some popular denials of the sovereignty of God in the salvation of sinners. Due to the prevalence of Arminianism among Fundamentalists, the denials about to be named are exceedingly prevalent. Many evangelists proclaim them, in spite of the fact that they do not contain a shred of good news. It is said that God owes every human being at least a chance at salvation. And it is said that God is unable to save a sinner unless the sinner permits him to do so. But a God who is indebted to sinners is hardly sovereign. And a God who is dependent on sinners is far from sovereign. The truth of the matter is that, while we owe God everything, he owes us nothing, and when God wills to save a sinner the first thing he does is to make the sinner willing to be saved, the sinner's willingness being not of himself but of God.

THE SOVEREIGNTY OF GOD AND HIS COMMANDMENTS

I was teaching Homiletics. One of my students was to prepare a sermon on the petition of the Lord's Prayer, 'Thy will be done on earth as it is in heaven.' He came to me for a bit of advice. He said, 'I have about come to the conclusion that the will of God spoken of in this text is his preceptive or revealed will, not his decretive or secret will. Do you think I am on good ground?' When I told him that likely he was, he inquired, 'Am I then to assume that this petition contains no reference to the divine sovereignty?' Now I had to inform him that he was wholly mistaken. This student made the common error of confining the sovereignty of God to his decretive will. The truth of the matter is that the divine sovereignty comes to expression also in his commandments. Whatever he commanded he commanded sovereignly.

Here a crucial question must be faced. Is a deed good because God commanded it, or does God command a deed because it is good? To say the latter is to assume that there is a norm of goodness which is outside of God and to which God is subject. And that is an obvious denial of the divine sovereignty. Conversely, to take the position that a deed is good because God commands it is to uphold the divine sovereignty. Yet it must be granted that the bare statement that a deed is good because God commands it, however true, lies open to the misinterpretation that, when declaring a deed good, God acts arbitrarily. As was said previously, divine sovereignty is not arbitrariness. A deed is indeed good because God commands it, and he commands it because he himself is good.

*

The doctrine of divine sovereignty is usually thought of as being extremely abstract. As a matter of fact its significance is intensely practical. It is for God's children to glorify God for his sovereignty by recognizing his guidance and government in each event and the whole of history; by, in our own experiences, thanking for prosperity the Father of lights from whom every good and perfect gift comes down [*Jas* 1:17], and in adversity trusting him who causes all things to work together for good to them that love him, even to them who are the called according to his purpose [*Rom* 8:28]; and, not to be forgotten, by keeping his commandments. Doing that, we shall be honouring God as God.

IV

Man is a responsible being

THE Bible throughout teaches emphatically that God is sovereign. The Bible throughout also teaches emphatically that man is a responsible being. Philosophers and theologians have striven hard to harmonize these teachings with each other, but have failed. To finite and sin-darkened human reason these truths seem irreconcilable. That is what we mean when we say that they constitute a paradox. The Bible contains many paradoxes. To be sure, Scripture never actually contradicts Scripture, but *seemingly* it often does.

It is a matter of the utmost importance, when confronting a scriptural paradox, to subject our logic to the divine *logos*, our reason to the Word of God. And that means that we must beware of rejecting either element of a paradox. It also means that we must be on our guard against softpedalling one element at the expense of the other. In short, we must make sure of doing full justice to both elements.

It will be shown that in this respect the Reformed faith excels.

THE BASIS OF HUMAN RESPONSIBILITY

The basic questions of all theology are *Who is God?* and *What is Man?* The Reformed answers to these questions constitute the basis for human responsibility.

God is the sovereign Ruler of the universe. His sovereignty is absolute. Shall we say that he is sovereignty personified? For that very reason man is responsible to him. We may not be able to harmonize divine sovereignty and human responsibility with each other, but it is safe to assert that the latter is a corollary of the former. If God were less than sovereign, man would be less than responsible. Since God is absolutely sovereign, man is wholly responsible to him. A theologian once said this: 'Calvinism stresses divine sovereignty, Arminianism stresses human responsibility.' A worse caricature is hardly conceivable. That Calvinism stresses divine sovereignty more strongly than does Arminianism is obvious. But precisely for that reason it stresses human responsibility more strongly than does Arminianism. Is it not the teaching of Arminianism that God never requires of man what he cannot do, but adjusts the demands of his law to the enfeebled powers of fallen man? According to the Reformed faith God makes no such concession. He keeps demanding of man whatever he was capable of in the state of rectitude. He requires of man not merely what has come to be known as 'evangelical obedience'; he insists on perfect obedience. He commands, 'Be ye perfect even as your Father which is in heaven is perfect' [*Matt* 5:48].

That man was created by God in his image and likeness is the teaching of *Genesis* 1:26, 27. This teaching, although not peculiar to the Reformed theology, is strongly stressed in that theology. The Reformed faith is often berated for its low view of fallen man. It does hold that fallen man is totally depraved. But the Reformed faith has a high view of man as created by God. It stresses the Scriptural teaching that he bears the divine image. That image makes man man. It follows, among other things, that man in his very nature is free. Such freedom is a prerequisite of responsibility. When in the Garden of Eden God gave to man the trial command, he was free to obey or to disobey. To be sure, God had foreordained that he would disobey, and so his fall was completely certain. To deny that is to deny the divine sovereignty. But to deny that man was free to sin or not to sin is to deny human responsibility. Paradoxical though they may be, both absolute divine sovereignty and full human responsibility must be upheld.

The fall of man seriously marred the image of God in which he had been created. In large measure he even lost that image. But he did not lose it completely. Vestiges of it remain in fallen man. He is still a free agent. To be sure, this does not mean that he has a free will in the sense that, when confronted with the choice between good and evil, he can as well choose the one as the other. His will is controlled by what Scripture calls his 'heart', the inmost disposition of his heart; and in the case of unregenerate man it is evil. 'The heart is deceitful above all things, and desperately wicked: who can know it?' [*Jer* 17:9]. 'The carnal mind is enmity against God: for it is not subject to the law of God, neither indeed can it be' [*Rom* 8:7]. Yet he is a free agent. That is to say, no outside force compels him to do either good or evil. Every time he sins, he sins because he wants to. And he has a sense of right and wrong, a conscience, which, however much distorted by sin, warns him against the doing of evil. The law of God written in man's heart from the beginning has not been entirely erased [*Rom* 2:15]. If it had been, he would no longer be a human being. As it is, he still is that. Therefore he is 'without excuse' [*Rom* 1:20]. And that is a way of saying that he is a responsible being.

MAN'S RESPONSIBILITY AND HIS ETERNAL DESTINY

The eternal destiny of every human being was determined by God in the decree of predestination. Some were predestined to eternal life, others were predestined to eternal death. And the divine decree is unalterable. By all the marks of human logic it would seem to follow that nobody is responsible for his eternal destiny. But the infallible Word of God emphatically teaches quite the contrary.

Faith in Christ is prerequisite to salvation. The Lord Jesus identified it with coming to him when he said, 'He that cometh to me shall never hunger; and he that believeth on me shall never thirst.' He went on to say, 'No one can come to me, except the Father which hath sent me draw him' [*John* 6:35, 44]. Saving faith, then, is a gift of God. But to the unbelieving Jews of his day Jesus said, 'Ye will not come to me that ye might have life' [*John* 5:40], and thus he laid the blame for their unbelief squarely at their own door.

When, in the night of the earthquake, the Philippian jailer asked Paul and Silas what he had to do to be saved, what was their reply? Did they say, 'Salvation belongs to God alone and there is nothing you can do about it'? Emphatically not. Did they say, 'Salvation is for the elect only; if you are one of them, you are bound to be saved; but if you are not one of them, you are helplessly lost'? They said nothing of the kind. Then did they say, 'Faith in Christ is the one requisite for salvation, but it is a gift which God sovereignly bestows on some and not on others'? If they had said that they would have uttered a truth, but it would not have been pertinent to the situation. What they did was to command the jailer to believe in Christ and to assure him that, if he obeyed that command, he would be saved [*Acts* 16:30, 31]. And, let it be noted, if a sinner truly desires to be saved, as did the jailer, God will not withhold the gift of faith from him. This very desire for salvation is evidence that the Holy Spirit has already begun a good work in his heart, a work which will certainly be completed.

God requires of those who have been born of the Spirit that

they believe, and they are sure to do so. God also commands unregenerate men to believe, and in so doing he demands of them a thing which they are utterly incapable of performing except they be first born again. This is often denied. Many say that a divine command implies the ability to obey on the part of him to whom the command comes. But thus great disservice is done to human responsibility. Man's responsibility goes far beyond his ability.

The Heidelberg Catechism has something to say on this matter. After teaching that unregenerate man is 'so corrupt that he is wholly incapable of doing any good, and inclined to all evil,' it asks, 'Does God, then, wrong man by requiring of him . . . that which he cannot perform?' And the answer is, 'Not at all; for God made man capable of performing it; but man, through the instigation of the devil, by his own wilful disobedience, deprived himself and all his posterity of these gifts' [See *Questions* 6–11]. How clear a case against man! God demands of man full trust and perfect obedience. As man came forth from the hands of the Creator he was obviously able to meet those demands. Through no fault of God, but 'by his own wilful disobedience,' he deprived himself of that ability. Surely, the divine demands stand. A farmer, let us say, bids his hired man plough a field and gives him strict orders to plough straight furrows. The hired man wilfully, through no fault of the farmer, drinks himself drunk. Now he cannot see straight, nor walk straight, nor, of course, plough straight. Obviously the farmer has the right to stand by his orders. The illustration is admittedly inadequate. God not only has the right to demand of fallen man full trust and perfect obedience; he persists in making those demands and threatens with eternal death all who fail to meet them.

The central teaching of the Canons of Dort is salvation by the sovereign grace of God. Do the Canons softpedal the responsibility of man? Most certainly not. Not in spite of, but precisely because of their insistence on divine sovereignty they strongly stress its corollary, human responsibility. The Canons teach that to God belongs *all* the credit for the sinner's salvation. That is their grand theme. They also teach that on the sinner falls *all* the blame for his damnation. 'Whereas many who are called by the gospel do not repent nor believe in Christ, but perish in unbelief, this is not owing to any defect or insufficiency in the sacrifice offered by Christ upon the cross, but is wholly to be imputed to themselves' [II, 6]. And 'it is not the fault of the gospel, nor of Christ offered therein, nor of God, who calls men by the gospel and confers upon them various gifts, that those who are called by the ministry of the Word refuse to come and be converted. The fault lies in themselves' [III–IV, 9].

It must indeed be granted that there are degrees of responsibility. Said the Lord Jesus, 'And that servant which knew his lord's will, and prepared not himself, neither did according to his will, shall be beaten with many stripes. But he that knew not, and did commit things worthy of stripes, shall be beaten with few stripes' [*Luke* 12:47, 48]. Yet it must be noted that even 'he that knew not' will be beaten, albeit with fewer stripes than 'that servant which knew his lord's will.'

Salvation is a momentary event. The new birth, which translates the sinner from death to life, occurs in the twinkling of an eye. But salvation is also a process which is completed only when the sinner has attained perfection. In regeneration the sinner is completely passive. In the process which follows he is a responsible agent. That is why the Bible commands Christians, 'Work out your own salvation with fear and trembling' [*Phil* 2:12].

To be sure, here too there are different degrees of responsibility. The Holy Spirit may well and, no doubt, often does regenerate such as are mentally deranged or emotionally disturbed, but it goes without saying that God does not demand of them what he requires of his children by and large. It is by no means a work of supererogation to warn believers generally against the evil of passivism or quietism. Not infrequently self-styled Calvinists become guilty of that sin. From the truth of their complete dependence on the sovereign grace of God for the whole of their salvation they conclude that they have no duty to perform with a view to salvation. They forget that the so-called fifth point of Calvinism, which is commonly called 'the perseverance of the saints', may also properly be denominated 'the perseverance of the saint'. The Bible assures the Christian that he who began a good work in him will perform it until the day of Jesus Christ [*Phil* 1:6], but also commands him, 'Be thou faithful unto death, and I will give thee a crown of life' [*Rev* 2:10]. He who stresses this assurance but spurns this command is not a Calvinist. Nor is he a Christian.

It is worthy of notice how Scripture relates the believer's responsibility in the process of his salvation to the sovereign grace of God. As was noted, *Philippians* 2:12 commands, 'Work out your own salvation with fear and trembling.' The very next verse reads, 'For it is God which worketh in you both to will and to do of his good pleasure.' Precisely *because* he is saved by sovereign grace the Christian is duty bound to work out his own salvation. And he is not merely told that such is his duty because it pleased God to bestow this sovereign grace on him in the past, namely, at the time of his regeneration. 'Worketh' is a present progressive tense. The Christian must work out his own salvation because God keeps working salvation in him. To his last breath he remains dependent on the sovereign grace of God for salvation. Because of the continued and continous operation of that grace within him, he must work out his own salvation. Again it becomes clear that human responsibility is a corollary of divine sovereignty.

How it behoves every child of God to make the prayer of Augustine his own: 'Lord, command what thou wilt; give what thou commandest.'

V

God is almighty

ALTHOUGH the Bible cannot be said to stress the divine omnipotence more strongly than it stresses such divine attributes as holiness and love, the truth that God is almighty looms exceedingly large in his self-revelation. So it does also in that confession of the faith of the historic Christian church which is known as the *Apostles' Creed*. Significantly, of all the divine attributes omnipotence is singled out for specific mention and it is named, not once, but twice. The church confesses its belief in 'God the Father *Almighty*, Maker of heaven and earth,' and in his Son Jesus Christ, who 'sitteth on the right hand of God the Father *Almighty*.'

By now, however, the doctrine of divine omnipotence has fallen on evil days. Not only is it being neglected, there are those who distort it, and not a few deny it. The present generation needs to be reminded of it.

THE BOUNDLESS POWER OF GOD

Omnipotence belongs to God alone. Only God is powerful to the point of being almighty. Time and again the Bible speaks of him as 'the Almighty'. In such Hebrew names as *El* and *El Shaddai* the idea of might is prominent. According to one etymology the same may be said of the name *Elohim*, and in this case the plural form brings out the fulness of divine power. The Old Testament tells us that nothing is 'too hard for Jehovah' [*Gen* 18:14; *Jer* 32:17], and in addressing Jehovah, Job said, 'I know that thou canst do everything' [*Job* 42:2]. The New Testament denominates God 'the only Potentate' [I *Tim* 6:15] and affirms that nothing is impossible with him [*Luke* 1:37]. Before God the statesmen, soldiers and scientists of earth, yea all nations, also the United Nations, are 'as nothing, and they are counted to him less than nothing, and vanity' [*Isa* 40:17]. He causes the wrath of man to praise him [*Ps* 76:10]. He will break his enemies with a rod of iron and dash them in pieces like a potter's vessel [*Ps* 2:9]. All the forces of the universe, atomic and hydrogen bombs included, are completely under his control. So are the sun and its planets, the moon, the stars in their courses, and the galaxies, vast beyond human imagination [*Isa* 40:26]. And the influence exerted by the grim prince of darkness on the affairs of men and nations is wielded by divine permission and divinely overruled for the good of God's people and the coming of his kingdom [*Rom* 8:38, 39].

God exercises his power in creation [*Ps* 33:6, 9] and in providence [*Heb* 1:3]; in the creation of the universe out of nothing, 'so that things which are seen were not made of things which do appear' [*Heb* 11:3], commonly called immediate creation, and in the creation, for example, of man's body from 'the dust of the ground' [*Gen* 2:7], sometimes called mediate creation; in such natural occurrences as the sending of rain [*Matt* 5:45] and such supernatural events known as miracles – the concurrence of natural factors not necessarily being excluded – as the crossing of the Red Sea by the Israelites with 'the waters a wall unto them on their right hand and on their left' [*Ex* 14:22]; in the resurrection of Christ from the dead [*Rom* 1:4] and in the entire process of redemption [*Eph* 1:19, 20; *Eph* 3:20; I *Pet* 1:5; II *Pet* 1:3, 4].

In each of his works and in all of them God manifests his omnipotence. It is worthy of special note that throughout Scripture salvation is ascribed to the power of God as well as to his mercy, grace and love.

Scripture ascribes to God, not only all might, but also all authority, all right, all competence, to exercise that might. The New Testament speaks of God's *exousia* [*Matt* 28:18] as well as his *dunamis* [*Matt* 6:13] and *kratos* [*Eph* 1:19]. To employ Latin terminology, it defines the divine power not only as *potentia* but also *potestas*. That fact bears directly on the proper understanding of the divine sovereignty. The sovereignty of God, which is hardly a divine attribute in the usual theological sense of that term, but a relation of God to his creatures and, according to some, a 'relative attribute', is primarily a matter of unrestricted right. The notion that might is right is not only foreign to Scripture, it is abominated by Scripture.

OMNIPOTENCE AND THE WILL OF GOD

The sentence *God can do what he wills*, embraces a pointed definition of the divine omnipotence. It is also a very exact statement of fact. God can do without any exception what he wills to do. To say that God cannot in the present or in the future do whatever he wills or that he could not do in the past whatever he would is to detract from his omnipotence; and, obviously, to detract from omnipotence is to deny it. God declares, 'My counsel shall stand and I will do all my pleasure' [*Isa* 46:10]. 'Our God is in the heavens; he hath done whatsoever he hath pleased' [*Ps* 115:3]. According to the consistent teaching of Scripture Nebuchadnezzar was completely right when he declared of the God of Israel, 'He doeth according to his will in the army of heaven and among the inhabitants of the earth; and none can stay his hand or say unto him, What doest thou?' [*Dan* 4:35].

Unassailable as the statement is that God can do whatever he wills to do, God cannot will what is contrary to his nature. The school of philosophy known as nominalism erred grievously when, divorcing omnipotence from the other divine attributes, it taught that God can err, sin, suffer and die. Thus, after the manner of Islam, it reduced the power of God to sheer arbitrariness and welcomed the pagan tenet that might is right. Scripture states explicitly that 'the Strength of Israel will not lie nor repent' [I *Sam* 15:29], that 'God cannot be tempted with evil' [*Jas* 1:13], that with him is 'no variableness, neither shadow of turning' [*Jas* 1:17]. It is obvious that the power of God is not thus restricted. The simple meaning is that the will of God in every instance reflects his perfection and is never contrary to his intrinsic excellence. When it is said of God, 'He cannot deny himself' [II *Tim* 2:13], this is to assert that he cannot cease being God, which means, among other things, that he cannot cease being omnipotent. To quote Augustine: 'The power of God is not diminished when it is said that he cannot die and cannot sin; for if he could do these things, his power would be less' [*De Civitate*, V, 10]. William G. T. Shedd says, 'God is not able to become non-existent. This would be finite weakness, not almighty power' [*Dogmatic Theology*, I, 360]. In short, the omnipotent God wills all that he wills and does all that he does because he is who he is.

The divine omnipotence is not exhausted by that which God does. Many prominent philosophers and theologians to the contrary notwithstanding, the actual is not co-extensive with the possible. To say that it is, amounts to confusing God and the universe, which is the essence of pantheism. To hold that God's power extends no farther than his will, is to make him no greater than his finite creation. God could have sent more than twelve legions of angels to prevent the Saviour's capture in Gethsemane [*Matt* 26:53], but it was not his will to do so. Scripture makes the amazing assertion that God is able of stones to raise up children unto Abraham [*Luke* 3:8]. Although there is no record of God's having done such a thing, he could have done it if he had so willed. In his standard work on Dogmatics Herman Bavinck says, 'God is not exhausted in the world, eternity does not empty itself into time, infinity is not identified with the sum of the finite, omniscience is not the same as the content of thought embodied in the creatures. Thus omnipotence is infinitely exalted above the boundless power revealed in the world' [II, 252f]. Again it becomes clear that the power of God is unlimited, that God is truly *omni*potent, that *absolute* omnipotence belongs to God. 'With God all things are possible' [*Matt* 19:26; *Mark* 10:27; *Luke* 18:27].

OMNIPOTENCE AND SALVATION

That the power of God extends beyond the will of God must be maintained in the interest of his sovereignty. While God's power is limitless, in the exercise of his power God is free. It is no less important to maintain that the free exercise by God of his power does not spell arbitrariness. Nothing can be more certain than that God will exercise his omnipotence in harmony with his nature. When the Saviour was hanging on the cross, the chief priests with the scribes and elders mocked him, saying, 'He saved others; himself he cannot save. If he be the King of Israel, let him now come down from the cross' [*Matt* 27:42]. They thought that he lacked the power to come down from the cross. In that they were mistaken. As the almighty Son of God he was abundantly able to do that. Yet, in a very real sense he who saved others could not save himself. He could not save himself precisely *because* he would save others. His determination to accomplish the task assigned to him by the Father and willingly assumed by himself fastened him to the cross. What made it impossible for him to come down from the cross was his love for sinners, his being what he was, namely love incarnate. It was not lack of power. In fact, his loving determination not to exercise the power which he had was itself an act of boundless power. Small wonder that he said, 'I lay down my life that I might take it again. . . . I have power to lay it down, and I have power to take it again' [*John* 10:17, 18]. His dying was an act of power as much as was his rising from the dead. That church-father was altogether right who imagined himself at the foot of the cross looking up to the dying Saviour and then exclaimed, 'Who is this that dies when he wills? To die is weakness; to die thus is power.'

Scripture teaches unmistakably the divine necessity of the atonement. This is not to say that the sovereignty of God is restricted. Nor does it mean that God is deficient in power. The Scriptural teaching of the divine necessity of the atonement detracts precisely nothing from the Scriptural teachings of absolute sovereignty and absolute divine omnipotence. The very nature of God demanded the sacrificial and substitutionary death of God's Son on the accursed cross. The Heidelberg Catechism says, 'By reason of the justice and truth of God, satisfaction for our sins could be made no otherwise than by the death of the Son of God' [XVI, 40]. If one may quote oneself, 'The God of infinite love is also a God of absolute justice and boundless wrath. At the dawn of human history the justice of God decreed that the ways of sin would be death [*Gen* 2:17; *Rom* 6:23], even death eternal. For God to depart a hair-breadth from the path of perfect justice would be to deny himself. But that is the one thing which God cannot do'

[*God-Centred Evangelism*, p. 156]. However, as was previously observed, God's inability to deny himself, instead of being impotence, spells omnipotence. Small wonder that Scripture ascribes salvation to the power of God and describes the gospel of Christ crucified as 'the power of God unto salvation' [*Rom* 1:16; 1 *Cor.* 1:18, 24].

DIVINE OMNIPOTENCE DENIED

Today the theory of evolution is widely accepted. Many substitute it for the account of creation found in Genesis 1 and 2. Others, denying that the Scriptural account of creation is actual history, attempt to harmonize it with evolution. Now in creation the divine omnipotence looms exceedingly large. Creation, whether immediate or mediate, is an act of the omnipotent divine will. Tampering with the Scriptural teaching of creation can only result in violation of the Scriptural doctrine of divine omnipotence. Here let it be noted that Scripture answers three basic questions to which the evolutionary theory has no answer whatever. These questions concern the origin of matter, the origin of life and the origin of man as a religious being. The Bible solves all three of these problems in terms of the divine omnipotence. Divine omnipotence created matter; divine omnipotence originated life; and divine omnipotence brought into existence that religious being who is known as man. Only God Almighty was able to effect these, and he did.

The divine omnipotence is displayed brilliantly in the supernatural. On that very issue today that which calls itself the Christian church is a house divided against itself. On the one hand, there are those who insist that supernaturalism is of the essence of Christianity; on the other hand, there are those who deny the supernatural and yet lay claim to Christianity. This cleavage goes back all the way to the apostolic age. The apostle John found it necessary to write a letter to the church members of his day in order to confirm their belief in the deity of Jesus [I *John* 5:13], and the apostle Paul contended with Hymenaeus and Philetus, who denied the future resurrection of the dead [II *Tim* 2:17, 18]. In the fifth century the church-father Augustine upheld supernatural salvation over against its denial by the British monk Pelagius. Although the Church of Rome adores Augustine, in its doctrine of salvation it has historically taken a mediating position between Augustinianism and Pelagianism. Today many leading churchmen deny the supernatural inspiration of the Bible, relegate the miracles of the Bible, among them the virgin birth of Jesus and his bodily resurrection, to the realm of mythology, and teach salvation by human effort instead of the grace of God. In his *Christianity and Liberalism* J. G. Machen demonstrated that the Modernism of his day was not Christianity but another religion. Cornelius Van Til has shown convincingly that the dialectical theology, often called neo-orthodoxy, is in reality a 'new Modernism'. Bishop James A. Pike has asserted that so far as the historic doctrine of the trinity is concerned he is an atheist. And Bishop John A. Robinson's *Honest To God* is a most blatant rejection of Christian supernaturalism and hence of Christianity.

When the Arminian, although accepting Christian supernaturalism generally, tells the sinner that God is impotent to save him without his consent, he too does violence to the Scriptural teaching of omnipotence. If he were to content himself with saying that it is not God's will to save sinners by external force or compulsion, he would not only be quite right; he would be stating a profound truth. As it is, he denies the Scriptural doctrine of efficacious grace. The grace by which the Holy Spirit quickens him who is dead in trespasses and sins is irresistible [*John* 3:3–6; *Eph* 2:1]. By the power of the Holy Spirit, operating within him, the sinner is rendered willing to be saved. His willingness, then, is a saving gift of God. 'It is not of him that willeth, nor of him that runneth, but of God that showeth mercy' [*Rom* 9:16].

PROPER CONTEMPLATION OF THE DIVINE OMNIPOTENCE

We human beings, even when we have put on 'the new man, which is renewed in knowledge after the image of him that created him' [*Col* 3:10], do not know all about God. We cannot know all about God for the obvious reason that the finite cannot comprehend the infinite. God being infinite, we finite beings must beware of speculating on his attributes, that of omnipotence included. For example, it has been said that the Son of God could have become incarnate without being conceived by the Holy Spirit and born of the virgin Mary. To be sure, here too it must be maintained that God could have done whatever he would. To deny that is to deny the divine omnipotence. Yet, what mortal has the right to assert dogmatically that the Word could have *willed* to become flesh in a way other than that in which he actually became incarnate? One safeguard against theological speculation is to refrain from isolating the divine attributes from one another. As a ray of white light, on passing through a prism, is broken up into the colours of the spectrum, so all God's attributes are manifestations of the one all-embracing divine attribute of perfection. In *Calvin and Calvinism* B. B. Warfield lauds the great Genevan for refusing in his *Institutes of the Christian Religion* to speculate on the divine attributes. He says, 'The divine power, righteousness, justice, holiness, goodness, mercy and truth are here brought together and concatenated one with the others, with some indication of their mutual relations, and with a clear intimation that God is not properly conceived unless he is conceived in all his perfections' (p. 170).

In the conclusion of his article 'Omnipotence' in the *International Standard Bible Encyclopedia* Geerhardus Vos makes the practical observation that the contemplation of the divine omnipotence ought to sustain our trust in God and evoke within us reverence for God. Rather than attempt to say the last word concerning omnipotence, it behoves us to accept in childlike faith its manifestations as related in the infallible Word, to trust God fully, also and especially in these turbulent times, for its exercise in the salvation of his own, the casting down of his enemies and the consummation of his glorious kingdom, and to adore God for his excellency, which, like all the divine excellencies, is infinite [*Westminster Shorter Catechism*, 4].

VI

The Love of God is infinite

'GOD is love' [1 *John* 4:8]. Exceedingly sad to say, that profound truth has often been misinterpreted. Both Ritschl and Schleiermacher singled out the divine attribute of love as the starting point of their theology. In consequence, present-day Modernism is wont to regard love as the very heart of the divine essence, and the other divine attributes as modes or manifestations of God's love. That holds of Barthianism also. Now such theology has no basis in Scripture. Beyond all doubt, all the divine attributes are the divine essence in the same sense. God is wholly righteousness and holiness as well as wholly love. However, that fact does not detract an iota from the truth that love is identical with the divine essence.

God is *The Infinite*. It follows that he is infinite in every one of his attributes. One of his attributes is love. The love of God, then, is infinite.

We human beings are finite. The finite cannot comprehend the infinite. We may indeed have knowledge, true knowledge, of the infinite, but our knowledge of the infinite is exceedingly far from exhaustive. In other words, in contemplating the love of God, or any other of his attributes, we are dealing with unfathomable mystery. Therefore it behoves us to subject our logic to the divine *logos*. The one and only question that should concern us is what the Bible has to say. And when that which

God tells us in the Bible concerning himself transcends our reasoning, we must humbly accept it as truth.

LOVE TRANSCENDING UNIVERSALISM

Infinity is often identified with universality. Not infrequently the two terms are used interchangeably. And so it is said that the love of God, being infinite, must embrace the universe and all it contains, every creature and the sum total of creation. Obviously that is an error. God created the angels but he does *not love* those angels who rebelled against him. Although the Bible tells us that those who failed to walk in God's way because they did not know it will be beaten with fewer stripes than will those who failed to walk in God's way although they knew it [*Luke* 12:47, 48], it nowhere intimates that God loves the damned. And, while the Bible teaches in its account of creation and elsewhere that God delights in the work of his hands, it stops short of saying that God loves mountains and valleys, rivers and oceans, earth and sky, plants and animals. It can safely be asserted that love by its very nature can be bestowed only on such objects as are capable of requiting it.

Let no one infer that universality transcends infinity. The exact opposite is true. Infinity transcends universality. And that truth is essential to the proper interpretation of that well-known but little-understood verse of Holy Scripture, *John* 3:16. God tells us here not merely that his love is great or even exceedingly great. He answers the question *how* great is his love. The significant, though little, word 'so' clearly indicates that. Now, of course, the one correct answer to that question is that the divine love is *infinite*. For that reason three professed interpretations of the term 'world' must be rejected. There are those who say that 'world' here means the elect, and that the love of God is so great as to embrace that countless throng. Others affirm that the love is greater than that, the term 'world' designating all human beings, whether elect or not. And there are those who insist that the love of God is far greater even than that, the term 'world' comprehending not only all men, but the sum total of things created, the whole of the universe. All three of these interpretations have a common fault. Every one of them represents an attempt to measure the infinite love of God in finite terms, which is something that simply cannot be done.

An illustration or two may clarify that point. Let us subtract a billion years from eternity. What is the remainder? Of course, it is eternity. But that is to say that a billion years in comparison with eternity is precisely nothing. Or let us imagine that you and I are visiting an old-fashioned blacksmith in his shop. The muscles of his arms are wonderfully well developed. I try to give you some idea of his great physical strength and so I say, 'This man is so strong that he can support a particle of dust in his extended palm.' What have I said? To be sure, I have said something very foolish, but I have said *something*. It takes at least a little strength to uphold even a dust-particle. But when I say that the love of God is so great as to embrace the countless throng of the elect, or the sum total of human beings, or the whole of the universe, I have said precisely nothing in terms of infinity. Even the universe is finite, and the sum total of finite things in comparison with infinity is nothing, and in the words of the prophet Isaiah, 'less than nothing' [*Isa* 40:17].

No doubt the term 'world' in *John* 3:16, as so often in the writings of John, is to be taken qualitatively rather than quantitatively. Plainly put, the emphasis is not on the size of the world, but on the sinfulness of the human race. To quote from a sermon on this point by that great American theologian,

B. B. Warfield, 'The key to the passage lies in the significance of the term "world". It is not here a term of extension so much as a term of intensity. Its primary connotation is ethical, and the point of its employment is not to suggest that the world is so big that it takes a great deal of love to embrace it all, but that the world is so bad that it takes a great kind of love to love it at all, and much more to love it as God has loved it when he gave his Son for it' [*The Saviour of the World*, pp. 120f]. God is holy, perfect in holiness. The very seraphs cover their faces because of his resplendent holiness and cry out to one another, 'Holy, holy, holy is the Lord of hosts' [*Isa* 6:3]. That holy God loves sinful humanity. All of Scripture contains no more profound teaching than that, nor one more incomprehensible. If you should tell me that, I would not believe it. If all men should tell me that, I would not believe a word of it. But now God tells me so in his infallible Word. The one thing for me to do is to bow my head in adoration and to stammer: 'I cannot understand, I do not begin to understand; but because thou, O God, sayest it, I believe.' Men have striven hard to describe the love of God adequately and have admittedly failed. They have said, 'If every man were a scribe, if every blade of grass were a pen, if the entire surface of the earth were paper and all the water in all the oceans were ink, it would be impossible for all those scribes with all those pens and all that ink on all that paper to describe the love of God.' Then they have sung in ecstasy,

O love of God, how strong and true!
Eternal, and yet ever new:
Uncomprehended and unbought,
Beyond all knowledge and all thought.

LOVE EMBRACING ALL LIVING MEN

Sad to say, there are those who stress the doctrine of divine election so as to rule out the love of God for all living men. They pride themselves in their Calvinism, but theirs is a kind of rationalism. Unable to square with their logic one plain teaching of the Bible with another just as plain, they do violence to the Word of God. Some of these have arrived at the absurdity that the rich young ruler, in spite of his refusal to obey the Lord Jesus, must have been numbered among the elect because, if he were not, Jesus would not have loved him, as the evangelist says he did [*Mark* 10:21].

Nothing could be clearer than the fact that the Bible speaks of a love of God for all living men. A few examples will suffice. The Psalmist sang, 'How excellent is thy lovingkindness, O God! Therefore the children of men put their trust under the shadow of thy wings' [*Ps* 36:7]. And in the Sermon on the Mount Jesus commanded, 'Love your enemies . . . that ye may be the children of your Father which is in heaven; for he maketh his sun to rise on the evil and on the good, and sendeth rain on the just and the unjust' [*Matt* 5:44, 45]. Obviously, we are here told that we must love all men, even our enemies, because our heavenly Father does.

The love of God for living men comes to expression in the blessings of nature. As Paul told the Lycaonians, 'He left not himself without witness, in that he did good, and gave us rain from heaven and fruitful seasons, filling our hearts with food and gladness' [*Acts* 14:17]. It comes to expression also and especially in 'the universal and sincere offer of the gospel'. God has commanded to proclaim the gospel to all men everywhere and he assures all to whom the gospel comes that he desires their repentance and salvation. Of course, we men, who do not know who are God's elect and who are not, must in all sincerity offer salvation to all men without distinction. Yet that is by no means the entire picture! The point at issue is that God, who does know who are the elect and who are not, in complete sincerity offers salvation to all to whom the gospel comes.

By the mouth of Ezekiel God declared, 'Have I any pleasure at all that the wicked should die, and not that he should return from his ways and live?' [*Ezek* 18:23]. On this passage Calvin commented, 'What the prophet now says is very true, that God wills not the death of a sinner, because he meets him of his own accord, and is not only prepared to receive all who fly to his pity, but he calls them towards him with a loud voice, when he sees how they are alienated from all hope of safety.... If any one should object – then there is no election of God, by which he has predestinated a fixed number to salvation, the answer is at hand: the prophet does not here speak of God's secret counsel, but only recalls miserable men from despair, that they may apprehend the hope of pardon, and repent and embrace the offered salvation. If any one again objects, 'this is making God act with duplicity,' the answer is ready, that God always wishes the same thing, though by different ways, and in a manner inscrutable to us. Although, therefore, God's will is simple, yet great variety is involved in it, as far as our senses are concerned. Besides, it is not surprising that our eyes should be blinded by intense light, so that we cannot certainly judge how God wishes all to be saved, and yet has devoted all the reprobate to eternal destruction, and wishes them to perish. While we look now through a glass darkly, we should be content with the measure of our own intelligence.'

The Canons of Dort teach unequivocally double predestination – election to eternal life and reprobation to eternal damnation. Significantly the Canons also assert, 'As many as are called by the gospel are unfeignedly called. For God has most earnestly and truly declared in His Word what is acceptable to Him, namely, that those who are called should come unto Him' [III–IV, 8].

In his standard work on Reformed Dogmatics Herman Bavinck, the prince of Dutch theologians, says, 'The offer of the gospel on the part of God is earnest and sincere' and 'Although through calling salvation becomes the portion of but few, as every one must admit, yet it has great value and significance also for those who reject it. For all without exception it is the evidence of God's infinite love and seals the word that he has no pleasure in the death of the sinner but therein that he turn and live' [IV, 6, 7].

In recent decades the love of God as expressed in 'the universal and sincere offer of the gospel' has been stressed by several noted Reformed theologians. Alexander De Jong has upheld it in scholarly fashion in a doctoral dissertation. Professors John Murray and Ned B. Stonehouse of Westminster Theological Seminary had previously done the same in a pamphlet entitled *The Free Offer of the Gospel*. It is a painstaking study of the Scriptural passages bearing on the theme. Much is made of II *Peter* 3:9: 'The Lord is not slack concerning his promise, as some men count slackness; but is longsuffering to usward, not willing that any should perish, but that all should come to repentance.' It is pointed out convincingly that the divine willing here spoken of has reference to men generally, elect and reprobate alike.

Throughout the history of the Christian church there have been those who inferred from the love of God for all men that there can be no such place or state as eternal hell. Today they are exceedingly numerous. But the logic of the Word of God is altogether different. There are men who accept the love of

God through faith in Jesus Christ, but there are also men who reject that love in unbelief. The latter sin grievously. And precisely because of the greatness of the love which they reject the just God will punish them severely. Let us suppose for the sake of argument that the divine love were small. In that case to spurn that love would be a relatively small sin. Now let us say that the love of God is great. That makes the spurning of that love a great sin. As a matter of fact the love of God is infinite. To spurn that love is a sin of infinite proportions. It calls for eternal punishment.

LOVE DIFFERENTIATING BETWEEN MEN

The Bible teaches clearly that God loves all living men. The Bible teaches just as clearly, and not a whit less emphatically, that the divine love differentiates between men.

God loves all men. Yet God hates 'all workers of iniquity' [*Ps* 5:5]. Whatever the precise context of the term *hate* may be in this connection, it is safe to say that God both loves and hates the workers of iniquity. But he loves the righteous without hating them. God has declared, 'Jacob have I loved, but Esau have I hated' [*Rom* 9:13]. Since God loves all men, he must have loved Esau too; but it is perfectly clear that he did not love Esau with the love with which he loved Jacob. In a real sense he hated Esau. Let no one obscure that truth by saying that God loves the wicked but hates their wickedness. The Bible tells us that God hates, not only the works of iniquity but its workers, that he hated not merely Esau's profanity, but Esau.

Here is mystery indeed, but mystery which is unmistakably taught in God's self-revelation. God forbid that we should lay down the law for the Most High by asserting that he cannot both love and hate the same person. God forbid also that we should attempt to analyse the Infinite and say that God has two different attributes both of which are called 'love' but one of which he manifests toward the wicked and the other toward the righteous. Of course, the love of God is one, but so are all his so-called attributes. The one all-embracing divine attribute is infinite perfection. As when a ray of white light shines through a prism it is broken up, so to speak, into the colours of the spectrum or the rainbow, so in God's self-revelation the divine perfection is manifested as omniscience, omnipotence, justice, holiness, love and numerous other attributes. God's attributes are diversified and yet add up to one. Small wonder that the one divine love is diversified!

The Bible differentiates between the love of God for men generally and his love for those who are in Christ. Of the many passages of Scripture which extol the special love of God for those who are in the Son of his love a few follow. The term 'foreknow' in *Romans* 8:29 means 'to love from eternity'. Those whom God loved from eternity 'he also predestinated to be conformed to the image of his Son that he might be the firstborn among many brethren'. And according to the following verse he further called, justified and glorified them. Paul informed the saints of Ephesus that God had chosen them in Christ before the foundation of the world, having predestinated them in love unto the adoption of children by Jesus Christ, to the praise of the glory of his grace wherein he made them accepted in the beloved [*Eph* 1:4–6]. To the same saints he wrote: 'God, who is rich in mercy, for his great love wherewith he loved us, even when we were dead in sins, hath quickened us together with Christ (by grace ye are saved), and hath raised us up together, and made us sit together in heavenly places in Christ Jesus, that in the ages to come he might show the exceeding riches of his grace in his kindness toward us through Christ Jesus' [*Eph* 2:4–7]. The same apostle gloried: 'I am persuaded that neither death, nor life, nor angels, nor principalities, nor powers, nor things present, nor things to come, nor height, nor depth, nor any other creature, shall be able to separate us from the love of God, which is in Christ Jesus our Lord' [*Rom* 8:38, 39]. *The Bible tells us that God loves those who are in Christ with the same love with which he loves his Son.*

Surely it is no wonder that the same Herman Bavinck who described as 'infinite' the love of God revealed in the universal and sincere offer of the gospel, also said unequivocally, 'One cannot and may not say that God has loved all men, at any rate not with that special love wherewith he leads the elect to salvation' [*Gereformeerde Dogmatiek* III, 530 and IV, 7]. Nor is it strange that Charles Hodge, that giant among American theologians, was wont to speak of God's people as a peculiar people whom God loves with 'a peculiar love' [*Systematic Theology* II, 550]. Nor yet is it surprising that Geerhardus Vos, meticulous scholar that he was, described the love which Paul had in mind when he spoke of 'the Son of God, who loved me and gave himself for me' [*Gal* 2:20] as 'love excelling' and 'love supreme' [*Dogmatiek* II, 152].

VII

Salvation belongs to the triune God

THE Bible teaches plainly and emphatically that there is but one God. Moses proclaimed, 'Hear, O Israel; the Lord our God is one Lord' [*Deut* 6:4]. The Bible teaches just as plainly and just as emphatically that there are three distinct divine persons. Paul exclaimed, 'Blessed be the God and Father of our Lord Jesus Christ' [*Eph* 1:3]. Toward the end of his version of the gospel John declared, 'These are written that ye might believe that Jesus is the Christ, the Son of God' [*John* 20:31]. And immediately after charging Ananias with lying 'to the Holy Ghost' Peter affirmed, 'Thou hast not lied unto men but unto God' [*Acts* 5:3, 4]. In the apostolic benediction [II *Cor.* 13:14] and in the baptism command [*Matt* 28:19] the three persons of the Godhead are, so to speak, placed on a par with one another. Such is the doctrine of the Holy Trinity.

That doctrine has fallen on evil days. Not only is it being denied outright by Unitarians, but also many leading Protestants brush it aside as pure speculation or worse. Among them is the well-known Episcopalian James A. Pike. And yet the doctrine of the Trinity is basic to the Christian religion. It is no exaggeration to assert that the whole of Christianity stands or falls with it.

The Apostles' Creed, known as the Creed of Christendom, consists of three parts: God the Father and our creation, God the Son and our redemption, God the Holy Spirit and our sanctification. At once it becomes clear that the doctrine of the Trinity not only upholds the Scriptural view of God but also refutes false conceptions of God. All conceptions of the Supreme Being can be subsumed under three heads: Pantheism, Deism and Theism. Pantheism identifies God and the universe, the Creator and creation. Deism tells us that God may indeed have created the universe but that he pays no further attention to it and, indeed, does not need to because it takes care of itself like a wound eight-day clock in your home when you leave for a week of vacation. Theism designates the biblical teaching concerning God. Now it is clear that the doctrine of 'God the Father and our creation' refutes Pantheism. Far from being identical with the universe God existed before the universe and brought it into being. It is equally clear that the doctrine of 'God the Son and our redemption' and the doctrine of 'God the Holy Spirit and our sanctification' have nothing in common with Deism and even teach its exact opposite. Instead of keeping himself aloof from the universe, God comes to dwell among men and even indwells certain men in order to save them. Theism, on the other hand, is identical with the biblical doctrine of the Trinity.

The same doctrine is woven into the very warp and woof of God's self-revelation in Holy Scripture. The entire content of Scripture may be summarized under these heads: man's creation, man's fall, and man's salvation. The Bible teaches that the triune God was active in creation. God the Father brought into being. He did so by the Word which became flesh [*John* 1:3, 14]. And the Spirit brooded, as it were, over creation, imparting life to it [*Gen* 1:2]. Likewise the Bible teaches that the salvation of fallen man is accomplished by the three persons of the Trinity.

Salvation belongs to the triune God

It follows that the doctrine of the Trinity, far from being speculative, is of the greatest practical importance. Nothing has greater practical significance than the salvation of sinners. The Scriptural doctrine of God and the Scriptural doctrine of salvation are inseparable and interdependent.

GOD THE FATHER SAVES

The Bible tells us that from eternity God in sovereign love chose certain persons out of the fallen human race unto eternal life [*Rom* 8:29, 30; *Eph* 1:4, 5).

That choice was unconditional and therefore unalterable. God did not decree, for instance, that certain persons would be saved if they should believe in Christ. 'According to the good pleasure of his will' [*Eph* 1:5] he decreed that they would be saved through faith in Christ. In other words, their election made their salvation certain. And that means that God the Father does not merely make salvation possible; he makes it actual. In short, God the Father saves. Scripture tells us explicitly, 'Whom he did foreknow [that is, love from eternity], he also did predestinate. Moreover, whom he did predestinate, them he also called; and whom he called, them he also justified; and whom he justified, them he also glorified' [*Rom* 8:29, 30]. It is completely certain that God will save his elect to the utmost. Once more, God the Father saves.

The Bible tells us that God chose *in Christ* those whom he chose unto eternal life. What is the meaning of the phrase *in Christ*? In his commentary Calvin suggests the answer when he says, 'If we are chosen in Christ, it is not of ourselves,' and 'the name of Christ excludes all merit and everything which men have of their own.' As Adam was the representative head of the human race, so Christ is the representative head of the elect. And as Adam's guilt was imputed to his posterity, so the merits of Christ are imputed to the elect. In fact, God had those merits in view in their election. That is to say, when God chose certain persons unto eternal life he did not do so in order that one day they might be in Christ, but he viewed them from eternity as being in Christ. And that means, to put it succinctly, that election is salvation. Let it be said again, God the Father saves.

In John 17 Jesus spoke of election without using the term 'election'. He described the elect as those whom the Father had given him. The Father gave them to the Son in order that he might save them. Therefore the Son prayed, 'Father, I will that they also whom thou hast given me be with me where I am, that they may behold my glory' [*John* 17:24]. The very act of giving, then, was an act of salvation.

Speaking of believers Jesus said, 'My sheep hear my voice, and I know them, and they follow me; and I give unto them eternal life; and they shall never perish, neither shall any man pluck them out of my hand.' But he did not stop there. He went on to say, 'My Father, which gave them me, is greater than all; and no man is able to pluck them out of my Father's hand. I and my Father are one' [*John* 10:28–30]. He ascribed the eternal security of believers to God the Father as well as to God the Son.

Having chosen his own in Christ and having given them to the Son, God the Father sent his Son into the world to effect their salvation. He also sent the Holy Spirit to the same end.

GOD THE SON SAVES

A term frequently used in Christian theology to describe the saving work of the Son of God is 'atonement'. According to Scripture Christ's work of atonement has two aspects – a negative and a positive. By what theologians call, somewhat unhappily, his passive obedience he paid the debt of sinners; by his active obedience he merited eternal life for sinners.

The English word 'passive' is derived from the Latin word for 'suffering'. In his suffering Christ was decidedly active. He suffered willingly for the sins of his people. 'He was wounded for our transgressions, he was bruised for our iniquities; the chastisement of our peace was upon him, and with his stripes we are healed. All we like sheep have gone astray; we have turned every one to his own way; and the Lord hath laid on him the iniquity of us all' [*Isa* 53:5, 6]. He paid the penalty of our sins not in part, but the whole. All of us are hell-deserving sinners, but in our stead he endured the agony of hell in the garden of Gethsemane and on the cross. 'It is written, Cursed is every one that continueth not in all things which are written in the book of the law to do them' [*Gal* 3:10]. That applies to every human being. But Scripture proceeds: 'Christ hath redeemed us from the curse of the law, being made a curse for us: for it is written, Cursed is every one that hangeth on a tree' [*Gal* 3:13]. When Christ was hanging on the cross darkness enveloped the whole land – him too. God was hiding his face from him. Aware of that fact, he cried out with a loud voice, 'My God, my God, why hast thou forsaken me?' [*Matt* 27: 45, 46]. That was very hell. Would you know what makes heaven heaven? It is communion with God. And would you know what makes hell hell? It is to be forsaken of God. That cry was one of hellish agony. When Christ uttered it, all the waves and the billows of the divine wrath against sin rolled over his head and crushed his soul; he was at the very bottom of the bottomless pit. Only thus could he atone in full for the sins of his people.

Imagine yourself without any assets and in debt to the extent of a million dollars. You have a friend who is both good and rich. He pays your debt to the last dollar. You surely have reason for profound gratitude, but just how rich are you now? Obviously you are not rich at all. Rather you are as poor as the proverbial church-mouse. Let no one think that the Saviour deals thus with those whom the Father has given him. To be sure, he pays their debt to the last farthing, but he also bestows upon them the infinite riches of life eternal. Those riches he merited by what is known as his active obedience, his perfect obedience to the law of God. By disobeying God Adam merited death for himself and all his descendants. If he had remained obedient, God would have rewarded him with eternal life. That is to say, he would have progressed to a state in which he could no longer sin and in consequence could no longer die. What the first Adam failed to do and what none of his descendants has been able to do, the last Adam, Jesus Christ, did. Throughout his earthly stay he rendered perfect obedience to God. He could challenge his most bitter foes, 'Which of you convinceth me of sin?' [*John* 8:46]. He was 'holy' and 'undefiled' [*Heb* 7:26]. That obedience God imputes to all believers. 'As by one man's disobedience many were made sinners, so by the obedience of one shall many be made righteous' [*Rom* 5:19].

Arminianism teaches that the atonement made salvation possible for all men, although actual for no man, and that it is for the individual to make his own salvation actual by of his own volition believing in Christ. But thus the atonement is seriously degraded, and so is the Saviour. Man is thus made his own saviour. The Bible teaches that Christ by the atonement actually saves all whom the Father gave him. Precisely that is the essence of what is often called the doctrine of the limited atonement but is more precisely described as the doctrine of particular or definite or efficacious atonement. Frequently that doctrine is misrepresented. The point of it is not so much that not all men are saved by the atonement –

although that too is true, as that all whom the Father gave to the Son, all the elect of God, all those who are to be saved, are effectively saved by the atonement. As the Canons of Dort put it, 'The death of the Son of God is the only and most perfect sacrifice and satisfaction for sin; and is of infinite worth and value, abundantly sufficient to expiate the sins of the whole world.' Also, 'whereas many who are called by the gospel do not repent, nor believe in Christ, but perish in unbelief; this is not owing to any defect or insufficiency in the sacrifice offered by Christ upon the cross, but is wholly to be imputed to themselves' [II, 3, 6]. Truly, Jesus saves. He does not give sinners a chance of salvation. He saves.

To be sure, faith in Christ is a prerequisite of salvation, but a most significant truth which is often overlooked is that faith itself is a fruit of the saving work of Jesus Christ. We owe to Christ *all* the benefits of salvation: not only the forensic benefits, such as forgiveness of sins and the title to eternal life, but also the ethical benefits such as regeneration, faith and conversion. The ethical benefits, bestowed by the Holy Spirit, were merited by Christ. That is what theologians have in mind when they say that Christ merited the Holy Spirit for his own. And the Bible tells us that Christ 'of God is made unto us wisdom, and righteousness, and sanctification, and redemption; that, as it is written, He that glorieth, let him glory in the Lord' [1 *Cor.* 1:30, 31]. Through Christ God bestows upon his own all the blessings of salvation. One of them is the gift of faith. Let it be said again, Jesus saves.

Let no one think that when Jesus breathed his last on the cross he ceased from his work as Saviour. It must be said emphatically that he did nothing of the kind. The resurrected and ascended Christ continues his saving work and will continue it until all the redeemed shall have entered through the gates into the celestial city. He poured forth the Holy

Spirit upon the church and thus empowered the church to preach the gospel to all nations. Thus he continues his activity as prophet [*Acts* 2:33]. As priest he intercedes for God's elect at the right hand of God [*Rom* 8:34]. As king he rules over his own and delivers them from the wiles of the devil [*Eph* 1:20–23]. And did he not say to his disciples, 'I go to prepare a place for you. And if I go and prepare a place for you, I will come again and receive you unto myself, that where I am ye may be also' [*John* 14:2, 3]? As he prepares a place for them, he prepares them for that place. One day he will return on the clouds, and at the sound of the trumpet will raise from earth and sea the bodies of those who have slept in him. Perfected souls will inhabit immortal bodies. 'Then will come to pass the saying that is written, Death is swallowed up in victory. O death, where is thy sting? O grave, where is thy victory?' [1 *Cor* 15:54, 55].

'Thanks be to God, which giveth us the victory through our Lord Jesus Christ' [1 *Cor* 15:57].

What a wonderful Saviour is Jesus our Lord!

GOD THE HOLY SPIRIT SAVES

The third person of the Trinity has correctly been called the Applier of salvation.

Salvation is both a momentary experience and a continuous process. Both are brought about by the Holy Spirit.

Regeneration, the new birth, the transition from spiritual death to spiritual life, is a momentary event, and he in whose life this event has taken place is a saved person. It is wrought by the Holy Spirit. Jesus said to Nicodemus, 'Verily, verily I say unto thee, Except a man be born of water and of the Spirit, he cannot enter into the kingdom of God. That which is born of flesh is flesh; and that which is born of the Spirit is spirit. . . . The wind bloweth where it listeth, and thou hearest the sound thereof, but canst not tell whence it cometh and whither it goeth; so is every one that is born of the Spirit' [*John* 3:5–8]. The regenerated person still needs to be saved. In this life he will not attain perfection. To the end of this life he will be in need of sanctification. B. B. Warfield was quite right when, as he often did, he would conclude his classroom prayers at Princeton Seminary with the petition, 'And save us all in the end for Jesus' sake. Amen.' Sanctification too, consisting of the mortification of the old man and the quickening of the new man, and affecting all the functions and faculties of the soul and even the body as temple of the Holy Spirit [I *Cor* 6:19], is the work of the third person of the Trinity. Paul thanked God for the brethren at Thessalonica because God had from the beginning chosen them to salvation 'through sanctification of the Spirit and belief of the truth' [II *Thess* 2:13]. And Peter addressed the saints in Asia Minor as 'elect according to the foreknowledge of God the Father, through sanctification of the Spirit, unto obedience and sprinkling of the blood of Jesus Christ' [I *Pet* 1:2].

In an important respect sanctification differs from regeneration. In regeneration the sinner is completely passive, in sanctification he is active. But this does not mean that sanctification is in part the work of the Holy Spirit and in part the work of man. All of it is the work of the Holy Spirit. Whatever contribution the believer makes to his sanctification, he makes under the control of the Holy Spirit. And when he heeds, as he must, the Scriptural exhortations to holy living, he does so by the grace of the Holy Spirit, who dwells within him.

It is by faith that men lay hold on Christ and his saving benefits. And that faith too is wrought in their hearts by the Holy Spirit. It is sad beyond words that this truth is being neglected by many fundamentalist preachers, even by so noted an evangelist as Billy Graham. They keep telling their hearers without distinction that it is within their power to believe in Christ and they keep assuring them that when they exercise that power they will be born again. The truth of the matter is that unregenerate man will not come to Christ that he might have life [*John* 5:40] and that only he who has been born of the Spirit is able to believe in Christ. The Bible tells us, 'The natural man receiveth not the things of the Spirit of God, for they are foolishness unto him; neither can he know them because they are spiritually discerned' [1 *Cor* 2:14]. Jesus identified coming to him with believing in him when he said, 'He that cometh to me shall never hunger; and he that believeth on me shall never thirst'; and, having done that, went on to say, 'No man can come to me, except the Father which hath sent me draw him' [*John* 6:35, 44]. God draws sinners by the Holy Spirit. Again the Bible assures us that 'no man can say that Jesus is the Lord, but by the Holy Ghost' [1 *Cor* 12:3].

Truly, God the Holy Spirit saves.

VIII

Salvation is by grace alone

THE Bible is the book of Salvation. God's general revelation in nature and history, valuable though it is, does not tell us how we may be saved from sin and its penalty; God's special revelation in the Bible tells us all we need to know on that all-important subject. Salvation is its central theme. It is salvation-centred.

The Bible is God's self-revelation. God is its central theme. It is God-centred.

The Bible is Christ-centred. Christ is its central theme. The Old Testament tells us that Christ is coming; the New Testament tells us that Christ has come and is coming again.

The three statements just made as to the central theme of the Bible are in no way contradictory. In fact, they are perfectly harmonious. That becomes clear when we acknowledge Christ as both God and Saviour and consider what it is that the Bible teaches concerning salvation. It teaches that salvation is of God and of him alone. For that is precisely what the Bible means when it tells us that salvation is by grace, and by grace alone.

This chapter, then, is nothing else than a continuation and elaboration of the immediately preceding. The title of that chapter was *Salvation belongs to the triune God*. The present chapter will emphasize the truth that salvation belongs to the triune God *alone*.

THE DOCTRINE IN SCRIPTURE

The great question is, and ever has been, whose work it is. Does God save the sinner or must the sinner save himself? Or is salvation a joint venture of God and man? It is no exaggeration to assert that according to the Bible salvation belongs to God a hundred per cent. No other interpretation does justice to the statement, 'By grace are ye saved through faith; and that not of yourselves: it is the gift of God' [*Eph* 2:8]. Again Scripture says, 'So then it is not of him that willeth, nor of him that runneth, but of God that showeth mercy' [*Rom* 9:16].

At once let it be noted that man has a responsibility in the matter of salvation. He must believe in Christ in order to be saved. Faith is a duty. When Paul and Silas said to the Philippian jailer, 'Believe on the Lord Jesus Christ, and thou shalt be saved' [*Acts* 16:31], they were not merely informing him that he would be saved if he believed; they were commanding him to believe. However, as has already been pointed out and will be stressed again, before faith becomes an act of man it is a gift of God. Likewise believers are commanded to work out their own salvation with fear and trembling, but they can do so only because it is God who keeps working in them both to will and to do of his good pleasure [*Phil* 2:12, 13]. *In short, whatever contribution men make to their salvation they make by the grace of God.* And that makes salvation the work of divine grace a hundred per cent. Charles Haddon Spurgeon was right when he said that, if there is to be in our celestial garment but one stitch of our own making, we are all of us lost. Or let us suppose that the work of salvation is a chain of ten thousand links. A chain is as strong as its weakest link. If but one link of the ten thousand is of the sinner's making, he is hopelessly lost. Then let us once and for all cease talking about God's part and man's part in salvation.

THE DOCTRINE IN HISTORY

Throughout its history the church of Christ has found it exceedingly difficult to maintain the truth of salvation by grace in all its Scriptural purity. It can hardly be said that all of the early church fathers had a perfectly clear insight into it, but in the fifth century the British monk Pelagius utterly rejected it. He taught that in so far as man needs salvation he himself is abundantly able to provide it. Over against the teaching of Pelagius the Biblical doctrine of salvation by grace alone was upheld by Augustine of Hippo. He was the author of two famous works, *The Confessions* and *The City of God*, but his *Anti-Pelagian Writings* are deserving of at least as much, perhaps even more, attention. A church council supported the teaching of Augustine. However, soon the church yielded to what has come to be known as Semi-Pelagianism. It held that the sinner can initiate the process of his salvation although he is unable to complete it without the help of divine grace. Came along the sixteenth-century Protestant Reformation. The Reformers generally, Calvin in particular, returned to the teaching of Paul and Augustine. The Scriptural teaching of salvation by grace was embodied in numerous Confessions. Sad to say, almost at once much of Protestantism weakened. In part it surrendered to Socinianism, which is essentially Pelagian, Lutheranism became identified with Synergism, and the Reformed churches had to contend with Arminianism. Both Synergism and Arminianism teach that because of man's inability he does indeed need the grace of God for salvation, but that God is dependent on man for its completion.

Today every one of the aforenamed departures from the

truth abounds. Among liberals Pelagianism is prevalent. It comes to expression in the popular lines of William E. Henley,

> *It matters not how strait the gate,*
> *How charged with punishments the scroll,*
> *I am the master of my fate;*
> *I am the captain of my soul.*

Roman Catholic theology is essentially Semi-Pelagian. Lutheranism adheres to Synergism. Arminianism is rife among Fundamentalists, who have the temerity to say that God is unable to save a sinner unless the sinner will let him. Most regrettable of all is the fact that few Reformed or Presbyterian communions consistently uphold the Calvinistic, the Augustinian, the Pauline, that is to say, the Scriptural doctrine of salvation by grace. The churches which do are few and relatively small. In other words, the so-called five points of Calvinism – total depravity, unconditional election, definite atonement, efficacious grace, and the preservation of the saints – which add up to salvation by grace alone, are exceedingly unpopular.

Meanwhile the Word of God keeps telling us that the natural man is not only sick, whether more or less, but dead, 'dead in trespasses and sins' [*Eph* 2:1], that only the grace of God Almighty can save him and that to his last breath he remains utterly dependent on that grace.

THE DOCTRINE IN PARTICULAR

It should prove reassuring to consider the doctrine of salvation by grace in a few of its details.

Basic to it is the doctrine of election. If a sinner is saved, the ultimate reason is that from eternity God chose him to life everlasting. One often hears it said that Arminius, the father of Arminianism, denied election; but that is not true. He taught election but distorted the teaching of Scripture on that subject. Instead of positing the sovereign good pleasure of God as the ground of election, as Scripture does when it says that God 'predestinated us unto the adoption of children by Jesus Christ to himself, according to the good pleasure of his will' [*Eph* 1:5], he held that the ground of election is the foreseen faith of the person elected. Thus he transferred the ground of election from God to man. What this teaching amounted to was that because of their worthiness God chose those whom he did choose. It is evident that serious violence was thus done to the truth of salvation by grace. You are a believer, let us say. God did not choose you because he knew that you would be a believer – although, of course he knew that; but you are a believer today because God chose you from eternity. Faith is a fruit of election, not the ground of it.

At this point an erroneous popular notion concerning election should be corrected. Many seem to think that it is extremely difficult, virtually impossible even, to discover whether one belongs to the elect. This is said to be one of the secret things which God has kept to himself. But this is not so at all. Faith as the fruit of election is also the proof of election. Therefore one can be just as sure of being numbered among the elect as he can be of being a believer.

Christ merited salvation for those whom the Father had given him. By his perfect obedience, obedience even unto death, he merited for them salvation *in full*. Nothing remains to be merited. That needs to be stressed.

Rome has always taught, and still teaches, the meritoriousness of good works. Liberal Protestantism teaches the same heresy with a vengeance. Rome holds that the sinner is saved by the merit of Christ plus the merit of the saints and his own; liberal Protestantism holds that the sinner is saved, in so far as he needs to be saved, by his own merit alone. But Jesus said, 'When ye shall have done all those things which are commanded you, say, We are unprofitable servants: we have done that which was our duty to do' [*Luke* 17:10]. Paul said, 'We conclude that a man is justified by faith without the deeds of the law' [*Rom* 3:28]. In accord with Scripture the Heidelberg Catechism answers the question why our good works cannot be even part of our righteousness as follows: 'Because the righteousness which can be approved of before the tribunal of God must be absolutely perfect, and our best works in this life are all imperfect and defiled with sin' [*Answer* 62]. And yet, some parents, professing loyalty to that catechism, tell their children to be good and assure them that, if they are good, they will go to heaven when they die; and then, when those children grow up, wonder where they became infected with the heresy of salvation by works. Even 'all our righteousnesses are as filthy rags' [*Isa* 64:6]. Therefore the believer sings and should teach his children to sing,

Nothing in my hand I bring,
Simply to thy cross I cling.

The notion is widespread that repentance merits the forgiveness of sins. To be sure, without heartfelt repentance there is no forgiveness, but this does not mean that repentance merits pardon. Buckets of tears would not suffice to blot out the guilt of a single sin. Only the blood of Jesus Christ atones for sin. Augustus M. Toplady was right when he confessed,

Could my zeal no respite know,
Could my tears for ever flow,
All for sin could not atone;
Thou must save, and thou alone.

The Roman Catholic Church has taught and still teaches –

although not as brazenly as formerly – that one can purchase the forgiveness of sins with money. Luther's famous ninety-five theses were directed especially against the sale of indulgences. As notorious a salesman as any was Tetzel. He assured the people that by gifts of money they could abbreviate the stay of dear ones in purgatory and could obtain for themselves forgiveness not only of sins committed but also of sins yet to be committed. Absurd though that teaching seems to us Protestants, the question may well be asked whether we have outgrown it. Is the thought altogether foreign to us that generous donations to Kingdom causes will help assure one of a place in heaven? Will the reader pardon a simple illustration? You went to the food store on Saturday. The person who checked you out gave you a dollar too much in change. You noticed the error but said nothing and pocketed the dollar. During the night your conscience began to trouble you. Before morning you decided to make up for your theft – for that it was – by depositing a hundred dollars in the Sunday morning offering. You actually did that, let us say. Did that atone for your sin? Of course not. And if you should assign all the goods of your house to the cause of Christian missions, even that would not begin to atone. Neither would hundred-fold restitution to the grocer make atonement. Christ atones, he alone.

At funerals it has become customary for us to eulogize the dead. And if the deceased was an active and prominent member of the church, we are wont to assign to him a high place in glory. I am confident that many Sunday School teachers go to heaven when they die. I have the same confidence as to elders. Being a minister myself, I am somewhat less confident concerning preachers. The Bible tells us in so many words that not nearly all of them will enter through the gate into the city. Did not Jesus warn, 'Many will say to me in that day, Lord, Lord, have we not prophesied in thy name?

.... And then will I profess unto them, I never knew you: depart from me, ye that work iniquity' [*Matt.* 7:22, 23]? Yet, no doubt, many a preacher too will be saved. But no one will be saved *because* he was a devoted Sunday School teacher, or a faithful elder, or an orthodox preacher. The most prominent member of the church will have to be saved as was the thief at Jesus' right hand on Calvary – by faith in the Christ crucified.

Not even by believing in Christ does one *merit* salvation. To be sure, the Bible tells us over and over again that we are saved by or through faith only, but nowhere does the Bible tell us we are saved *on account of* our faith. Christ merited salvation, the whole of it.

But the sinner must believe in Christ in order to be saved. And, to put the matter bluntly, nobody, not even God, is going to do the believing for him. Does it then follow that while the meriting of salvation is the work of Christ, the appropriating of salvation is the work of man? If so, in the last instance man becomes his own saviour and salvation is no longer of grace. But such is not at all the case. In fact, nothing could be farther removed from the truth. As was stated in the foregoing chapter, before faith becomes an act of man it is a gift of God the Holy Spirit.

What was said there may well be reinforced with Scripture here. Paul wrote to the Ephesian Christians, 'By grace are ye saved through faith; and that not of yourselves: it is the gift of God.' Whether the antecedent of 'it' is 'faith' or salvation by grace through faith, in either case it is taught here that faith is a gift of divine grace. And the same apostle told the believers at Philippi, 'Unto you it is given in the behalf of Christ, not only to believe in him, but also to suffer for his sake' [*Phil* 1:29]. To believe in Christ as well as to suffer with him is a gift of God.

Salvation is by grace alone

May I become personal? My lot has frequently been cast with Arminian Christians. Often I have argued with them. In the process I have sometimes put the question to them, 'Who deserves the credit for your being a believer – you or God?' Almost invariably the answer was, 'God, and God alone', which goes to show that at heart every believer accepts the Scriptural truth of salvation by grace alone. As B. B. Warfield has said in the article 'Calvinism' in *The New Schaff-Herzog Encyclopedia of Religious Knowledge*: 'Whoever believes in God; whoever recognizes in the recesses of his soul his utter dependence on God; whoever in all his thought of salvation hears in his heart of hearts the echo of the *soli Deo gloria* of the evangelical profession – by whatever name he may call himself, or by whatever intellectual puzzles his logical understanding may be confused – Calvinism recognizes as implicitly a Calvinist, and as only requiring to permit these fundamental principles – which underlie and give its body to all true religion – to work themselves freely and fully out in thought and feeling and action, to become explicitly a Calvinist.' To express the same truth differently, and for many more acceptably, every true Christian in his heart of hearts trusts in God alone for salvation. In fact, that constitutes him a Christian. How right Christina G. Rossetti was when she wrote,

Can peach renew lost bloom,
Or violet lost perfume,
Or sullied snow turn white as over-night?
Man cannot compass it, yet never fear:
The leper Naaman
Shows what God will and can.
God who worked there is working here;
Wherefore let shame, not gloom, betinge thy brow;
God who worked then is working now.

God the Holy Spirit can even make dead sinners alive and turn an unbeliever into a believer. He alone is able.

THE DOCTRINE IN PRACTICE

Likely no other book has been abused as has the Bible, and no other Biblical teaching has been abused as has the doctrine of salvation by grace. Already in the apostolic age there were those who made the deduction, 'Let us do evil that good may come.' Some went so far as slander to ascribe that deduction to Paul. But of these the apostle affirmed that their 'damnation is just' [*Rom* 3:8]. In the subsequent history of the Christian church, particularly of the Reformed churches, this doctrine has been used as a cover-up for Quietism and even Antinomianism. That is to say, men have deduced from the doctrine of salvation by grace that man can well be entirely passive in the entire process of his salvation and is under no obligation to obey the law of God. Thus they made the blasphemous blunder of placing Scripture over against Scripture.

In all the Word of God there is no doctrine which, if properly applied, is more conducive to godly living than is the doctrine of salvation by grace, and by grace alone. Let me try to make that clear in a simple way. Let us suppose that God performed fifty per cent of my salvation and I accomplished the other fifty per cent. Then, obviously, I would owe to God fifty per cent of what I am and have and I might well retain the remaining fifty per cent for myself. Now let us suppose that God performed ninety per cent of my salvation and I myself contributed the remaining ten per cent. Then, it is clear, I would owe to God ninety per cent of what I am and have and I might well retain the balance of ten per cent for myself. But the fact is that God has saved me a hundred per cent. It follows inescapably that I owe to God *all* I am and *all* I have.

Thus it becomes clear that the doctrine of salvation by grace alone is conducive *par excellence* not only to godly living on the part of the believer but also to the glorification of God, his Saviour.

Perhaps you will have a death-bed. You are conscious, let us say, and fully aware of the approaching end. What will you do? I am told that a person in that position is likely to review his life in retrospect. As you do that, to what conclusion will you come? Will you say to yourself, and perhaps to the bystanders, that you have lived so good a life that the gates of heaven must be standing wide open for you? Not if you are a Christian. More likely you will want read to you a penitential Psalm, as did the church-father Augustine. Your sins will rise up against you as a veritable mountain threatening to crush you. But the Saviour will be at your side and say, 'Fear not; put your trust in me.' You will whisper:

Just as I am, without one plea,
But that thy blood was shed for me,
And that thou bidd'st me come to thee,
O Lamb of God, I come, I come!

Your eyes will break in death. The next moment you will open them in the palace of the King and will see the King in his glory. A crown of gold will be given you but you will cast it at the feet of him that sits on the throne and exclaim, 'Not unto me, not unto me, but unto thee alone be glory and honour, for by thy grace was I saved.' And you will adore the triune God world without end.

IX

Salvation is by faith alone

CHRISTIAN theology speaks of saving faith. This is not to deny that God, and God alone, saves. What is meant is that faith is the instrumentality by which God saves.

True faith unites the sinner with Christ, the Saviour. Hence he partakes of Christ himself and of all his saving benefits. To use an admittedly inadequate illustration – the passenger-carrying coach of a train is joined by a coupling to the locomotive. The locomotive, not the coupling, pulls the train; yet without the coupling the passengers would not reach their destination. Thus Christ brings sinners to heaven by faith in him.

THE DISTINCTIVENESS OF SAVING FAITH

According to Scripture not all faith is saving faith.

There is such a thing as historical or speculative faith. It is identical with dead orthodoxy and consists of a cold intellectual acceptance of the truths of Scripture without a preceding change of heart or a subsequent and consequent change of life. Herod Agrippa II had it. Paul flung the challenge at him: 'King Agrippa, believest thou the prophets? I know that thou believest' [*Acts* 26:27]. But he kept living with his sister Bernice as his wife and was not converted to Christianity. Even demons possess that kind of faith. During Jesus' public ministry they often confessed him to be the Son of God. When casting out demons he did not permit them to speak 'because they knew him' [*Mark* 1:34]. And James warned his readers, 'Thou believest that there is one God; thou doest well; the devils also believe and tremble' [*Jas* 2:19]. Only God knows how much of this sort of faith is present in the church today. It comes to expression in sheer traditionalism.

In Bible times there were a great many instances of miraculous faith. It may be defined as a conviction that one can perform a miracle or that a miracle is to be performed for one's benefit. Jesus was wont to demand faith of those who requested miracles of healing [e.g., *Luke* 8:50], but it is by no means certain that all who were benefited by his healing power believed on him unto the salvation of their souls. Judas Iscariot was one of the twelve whom Jesus commissioned not only to preach the gospel, but also to heal the sick, to cleanse lepers, to raise the dead and to cast out demons [*Matt* 10:8], but Judas was 'a devil' [*John* 6:70].

In that parable which some call 'the parable of the seed' and others 'the parable of the soil', but which Jesus himself described as 'the parable of the sower' [*Matt* 13:18], mention is made of temporary faith. Said Jesus, 'He that received the seed into stony places, the same is he that heareth the word, and anon with joy receiveth it; yet hath he not root in himself, but dureth for a while: for when tribulation or persecution ariseth because of the word, by and by he is offended' [*Matt* 13:20, 21]. It is a shallow religious experience, involving the emotions but not rooted in the heart. It is a response to the Word with joy rather than sorrow for sin and heartfelt repentance. It is a hasty acceptance of the gospel which does not last under trial.

Saving faith differs radically from all three of the foregoing. As good a definition of it as any is given by the Heidelberg

Catechism: 'True faith is not only a certain knowledge, whereby I hold for truth all that God has revealed to us in His Word, but also a firm confidence which the Holy Spirit works in my heart by the Gospel, that not only to others, but to me also, remission of sins, everlasting righteousness and salvation are freely given by God, merely of grace, only for the sake of Christ's merits' [VII, 21].

SOME PREREQUISITES OF SAVING FAITH

As was demonstrated previously in these essays, the chief prerequisite of saving faith is regeneration. The spiritually dead sinner will not and cannot believe in Christ. He loves death rather than life [*Prov* 8:36] and will not come to Christ that he may have life [*John* 5:40]. Only when the Holy Spirit has given one a heart of flesh for a heart of stone does saving faith become possible. Then it is also bound to become reality.

Regeneration has certain effects which are likewise prerequisites of saving faith. For practical purposes two may be singled out. They are knowledge of Christ and conviction of sin.

Ours is an age of anti-intellectualism in religion. We are told that the less knowledge one has the simpler and stronger one's faith is going to be. Extremely prevalent is the utterly erroneous notion that faith begins where knowledge ends. Not infrequently saving faith is described as a leap in the dark. Following is the illustration sometimes used to make that point. A certain house has a basement. The only entrance to the basement is a trap door, and the only light that falls into the basement is that which comes through that door when it stands open. One day the father of the family occupying that house is working in the basement. His little daughter is playing around the open trap door. He can see her in the light, but she can see him only faintly, if at all, in the dark. He tells her to jump through the door and assures her that he will catch her. She obeys instantly and, of course, is caught in her father's strong embrace. As that little girl made a leap in the dark, we are told, he who believes in Christ makes a leap in the dark. Perhaps the illustration is better than it is intended to be. Did the little girl really make a leap in the dark? In a sense she did; in another sense she did nothing of the kind. She knew her father; she recognized his voice; she had experienced his love. Precisely her knowledge of her father accounted for what she did. Likewise, knowledge of Christ accounts for faith in him. No doubt Paul had that in mind when he asked the rhetorical question, 'How then shall they call on him in whom they have not believed? And how shall they believe in him of whom they have not heard? And how shall they hear without a preacher?' He drew the conclusion: 'So then faith cometh by hearing, and hearing by the word of God' [*Rom* 10:14, 17].

He who is born again will not only want to know what the Bible teaches concerning Christ, he will also assent to those teachings. And his assent will, to be sure, be intellectual, but more than that. It will spring from his renewed heart, his inmost being, the dominating disposition of his soul, from which are all the issues of his life [*Prov* 4:23]. Whether that assent is regarded as a prerequisite of saving faith or as one of its elements matters little. The important truth to remember is that without it there is no such thing as saving faith.

What are some of the Scriptural truths concerning Christ which one must know and to which one must assent in order to believe in him? It is well to know *all* that the Bible reveals about him, but it is questionable whether the greatest theologian does. No doubt there are depths in the Biblical revelation of Christ which no theologian, however learned, has ever fathomed. Knowledge of and assent to some truths, however, is indispensable. For example, one cannot believe in Christ unless one is convinced that Christ is God, for the Christ of Scripture is God, and any other Christ is non-existent. Besides, to trust for salvation in a merely human Christ is to bestow divine honour on a man, and this is idolatry. It is also inconceivable that one would trust in Christ unto salvation without knowledge of and assent to the Scriptural teaching of his vicarious death and triumphant resurrection. Does not the Bible tell us that he 'was delivered for our offences and was raised again for our justification' [*Rom* 4:25]? All in all, the more knowledge one has concerning the Saviour, the stronger one's faith in him can be.

When one is born of the Spirit one does not suddenly become perfect or even nearly so. Rather, one becomes exceedingly sinful in one's own estimation. That is to say, one comes under conviction of sin. That too is a prerequisite of saving faith.

John the Baptist, who prepared the way before the Christ, preached repentance. So did Christ himself. And so did the prophets and the apostles. The reason for the prominence of the call to repentance in Scriptural preaching is obvious. Conviction of sin is an indispensable prerequisite of faith in Christ. Just as one will not go to a physician unless he feels ill, so one will not flee to the Physician of souls unless he is burdened by sin. Only he who can say from the heart,

Naked, come to Thee for dress,
Helpless, look to Thee for grace;
Foul, I to the fountain fly;
Wash me, Saviour, or I die,

will commit himself to Christ for salvation. Only he who has cried with the publican of the parable, 'God be merciful to me a sinner' [*Luke* 18:13] and has confessed with the prodigal son of another parable, 'Father, I have sinned against heaven and in thy sight, and am no more worthy to be called thy son' [*Luke* 15:21], will abandon himself to the Christ crucified. And that holds for children of the covenant as well as for drunkards and prostitutes. For good reason the Heidelberg Catechism in answering the question, 'How many things are necessary for you to know, that you . . . may live and die happily?' makes mention first of all of 'how great my sin and misery are' [1, 2]. Only a repentant sinner can appreciate the love of God in Christ Jesus. Only he who can say, 'The sorrows of death compassed me and the powers of hell got hold upon me' will call upon the Lord for deliverance and, having been delivered, will extol the divine grace and mercy and exclaim, 'I love the Lord' [*Ps* 116:1–8].

THE ESSENCE OF SAVING FAITH

Just what is saving faith? On that important matter there is much confusion. The answer should be unmistakably clear. Let us, then, try to put into practice the old saying that he who distinguishes well teaches well.

In this connection the distinction between *proposition* and *person* is of very great importance.

The Bible teaches many propositions concerning Christ. To name a few, it tells us that he existed from eternity, for which reason he could say, 'Before Abraham was, I am' [*John* 8:58]; that he was conceived by the Holy Spirit and born of the virgin Mary [*Matt* 1:18–25, *Luke* 1:26–38]; that at the close of a public ministry of some three years he was crucified; that he was raised from the dead and after forty days ascended into heaven.

There are those who drive a wedge between these propositions concerning Christ on the one hand and the person of Christ on the other. They tell us that it makes little difference, if indeed any, whether one believes these propositions if only one believes in the person of Christ. Greater folly is hardly imaginable. These propositions define the person of Christ as well as his work; therefore he who rejects them rejects him. Nothing could be more obvious than that one cannot believe in the Christ of Scripture without believing the Scriptural propositions about him.

On the other hand, it is conceivable that one might accept the Scriptural propositions concerning Christ without committing oneself to the person of Christ for salvation. Precisely that is done by him who has only speculative or historical faith. He is orthodox, but his orthodoxy is of the dead kind. It is orthodoxism. Saving faith is the abandoning of oneself for salvation to the *person* of the crucified and resurrected Christ as revealed in Holy Writ. Precisely that is its very essence.

If in determining the essence of saving faith it is important to distinguish between propositions concerning Christ and the person of Christ, it is no less important to differentiate between the essence of faith and the assurance of faith.

It is not at all unusual for evangelists to identify the two. They say that to believe in Christ is to know for a certainty that Christ is one's Saviour. But such language is, to say the least, confusing. To be sure, saving faith always carries with it a measure of assurance, but it is not in every instance accompanied by full assurance. One may well be a believer without being able to say every hour of the day and every minute of the hour, 'I know that my redeemer liveth' [*Job* 19:25]; 'I know whom I have believed' [II *Tim* 1:12]; 'I am positive that when I die I am going to heaven.' Perfect faith would, no doubt, yield perfect assurance; but all that a child of God does is imperfect, even his believing.

Salvation is by faith alone

Let it then be said again, especially in the interest of babes in Christ and, for that matter, for the comfort of every Christian, the essence of saving faith is the abandonment of oneself for salvation to the Christ of Scripture.

One thought must needs be added. The Westminster Shorter Catechism defines faith in Christ as 'a saving grace whereby we receive and rest upon him *alone* for salvation' [*Q. and A.* 86; italics by R. B. K.]. The true believer says:

Nothing in my hand I bring,
Simply to thy cross I cling.

He sings:

Just as I am, without one plea
But that thy blood was shed for me,
And that thou bidd'st me come to thee,
O Lamb of God, I come, I come!

He exclaims:

None other Lamb, none other Name,
None other Hope in heav'n or earth or sea,
None other Hiding-place from guilt and shame,
None beside thee!

THE PROOF OF THE SAVING FAITH

Scripture teaches most emphatically that salvation is by faith alone, not by works. Paul said in so many words, 'We conclude that a man is justified by faith without the deeds of the law' [*Rom* 3:28]. Referring to the father of believers he went on to argue, 'For if Abraham were justified by works, he hath whereof to glory; but not before God. For what saith the scripture? Abraham believed God, and it was counted unto him for righteousness. Now to him that worketh is the reward not reckoned of grace, but of debt. But to him that worketh not, but believeth on him that justifieth the ungodly, his faith is counted for righteousness' [*Rom* 4:2–5].

It has sometimes been said that in his epistle James, the brother of the Lord, contradicted the aforesaid teaching of the apostle Paul. At first blush that would seem to have been the case. Did he not say, 'Ye see then how that by works a man is justified, and not by faith only' [*Jas* 2:24] It was for this reason that Martin Luther, who strongly stressed justification by faith only over against the Romish error of the meritoriousness of good works, at one time spoke of the epistle of James as 'an epistle of straw'. However, subsequently he changed his mind on that score. It is obvious that he did so for good reason. Careful study shows that Paul and James were in full agreement. James emphasized the truth that 'faith without works is dead' [*Jas* 2:26]; in other words, that saving faith is bound to prove itself in works, and that only such faith as does prove itself thus is worthy of its name. Nothing could be clearer than that, when Paul taught salvation by faith only, he had in mind precisely such faith. Said he, 'There is therefore now no condemnation to them which are in Christ Jesus, who walk not after the flesh, but after the Spirit' [*Rom* 8:1].

It has been suggested that Jesus, in his description of the final judgment, taught salvation by works. Will not the King say to those on his right hand, 'Come, ye blessed of my Father, inherit the kingdom prepared for you from the foundation of the world: for I was an hungred, and ye gave me meat: I was thirsty, and ye gave me drink: I was a stranger, and ye took me in: naked, and ye clothed me: I was sick, and ye visited me: I was in prison, and ye came unto me' [*Matt* 25:34–36]? However, this very passage teaches plainly that salvation is of grace. The redeemed will be addressed as 'blessed of my

Father'. They are what they are because God has seen fit to bless them. They are invited to 'inherit' the Kingdom. An inheritance is a gift, not something earned. And their inheritance was prepared for them 'from the foundation of the world', long before they came into being, even from eternity, when only God was. How clear that Paul's description of the elect is applicable to them: 'For we are his workmanship, created in Christ Jesus unto good works, which God hath before ordained that we should walk in them' [*Eph* 2:10]!

The Bible tells us unmistakably that salvation is by faith only, not by works. But nowhere does the Bible tell us that salvation is by a faith that does not work. Contrariwise, the Bible tells us emphatically that salvation is only by a working faith. In short, good works are the fruits of saving faith. They are also the proof of saving faith.

And good works are works of love – love for God above all else, love for those of the household of faith, love for all men, love even for enemies. Salvation is by faith alone, by such faith as 'worketh by love' [*Gal* 5:6].

X

Christianity is the one true religion

TIME was when ministers in Christian churches, professors in Christian schools of theology, Christian missionaries and evangelists proclaimed Christianity as the one true religion. Today the view is becoming more and more prevalent among those who would be known as Christians that Christianity is in a class – perhaps at the head of the class – with the many religions of the world. But the Bible teaches unmistakably that Christianity is the one and only true religion and that all other religions are essentially false.

This is not to say that other religions do not contain elements of truth. It would indeed be strange if they did not. Man was created in the image of God, consisting of true knowledge of God, righteousness and holiness [*Gen* 1:26, *Eph* 4:24, *Col* 3:10]. That is to say, man was created a religious being and his original religion was the true religion. But man was corrupted by sin and so was his religion. Every one of the ethnic religions, then, is a corruption of the original true religion. Would it not be surpassing strange if any one of them were so thoroughly corrupted that not a shred of truth remains in it? Besides, every religion under the sun has been influenced by God's general revelation in nature and history and by what the Reformed theology calls the common grace of God.

And so we find that all religions have certain beliefs in

common. They all profess belief in a supreme being and in a future life for man. Likewise every religion has a cult, and all religions have certain rites or practices in common: prayer and sacrifice. Every religion, too, insists on some kind of morality. Significantly, the apostle Paul, in preaching Christianity to the pagan Athenians, appealed to a true element in their religion. Said he, 'As certain also of your own poets have said, For we are also his offspring. Forasmuch then as we are the offspring of God, we ought not to think that the godhead is like unto gold or silver or stone, graven by art and man's device' [*Acts* 17:28, 29]. Well may today's Christian missionary follow suit. The truths in other religions afford valuable points of contact.

And yet, as was said, the Bible insists that Christianity is the one and only true religion and that all other religions are essentially false. Christianity has the only true Word; the 'sacred books' of other religions deceive. Christianity has the only true God; all other gods are idols. Christianity has the only true Saviour; every other saviour so called leaves and leads men to destruction. Christianity has the only true morality; no other religion conduces to true holiness.

All that, let it be said emphatically, constitutes compelling reason for the zealous propagation of Christianity throughout the world.

THE ONLY TRUE WORD

Many religions lay claim to 'sacred books'. To name but a few, the Chinese have their five Ching and their four Shu; the Hindus their Vedas, Brahmanas and several others; the Buddhists their Tripitaka; the Mohammedans their Koran; the Mormons their Book of Mormon. All of these express the wisdom of men; some excel in that wisdom; but without exception they are exceedingly fallible.

In that respect Judaism would seem to be exceptional. It claims to be based on the divinely inspired Old Testament. However, by its rejection of the New Testament, in which alone the Old is patent, Judaism gravely distorts divine revelation, and by spurning Jesus of Nazareth as Messiah it spurns the Messiah of the Old Testament as well as the New. What Paul said of the Jews of his day remains true of the present-day adherents of Judaism: their minds are 'blinded'; there is 'a veil . . . upon their heart'; it remains 'untaken away in the reading of the Old Testament' [II *Cor* 3:14, 15].

Of all the religions of the world Christianity alone is based upon the Bible, which 'given by inspiration of God' [II *Tim* 3:16] is God's inerrant and infallible Word.

There exists the closest relationship between the written Word, the Bible, and the personal Word, Jesus Christ. The personal Word is the author of the written Word; he is also its theme, the Old Testament saying that he is going to come, the New that he has come and is coming again. The written Word informs us that the personal Word has affirmed that he is 'the Truth' [*John* 14:6] and that he has declared no less emphatically that the written Word is 'truth' [*John* 17:17].

How clear that Christianity – it alone of all religions – is rooted in the only true Word of God!

THE ONLY TRUE GOD

Moses declared, 'Hear, O Israel: the Lord our God is one Lord' [*Deut* 6:4]. 'Thou art God alone,' said the Psalmist [*Ps* 86:10]. God himself commanded, 'Thou shalt have no other gods before me' [*Ex* 20:3, *Deut* 5:7].

Not only does a passage here and there in the Bible assert

that the God of the Bible, who is the God of Christianity, is the only true God; the testimony of the entire Bible is that the God who has revealed himself in it is God alone.

The God of the Bible is unique, not merely in *some* respects, but in *all*. A candidate for the ministry was being examined. The question was put to him, 'How does the God of Christianity differ from the gods of other religions?' The candidate answered, 'In that he is one.' The questioner was not satisfied. He objected, 'But the Jews also recognize but one God, Jahweh; and so do the Mohammedans, namely Allah.' So the candidate thought once more and now said, 'In that he is triune.' This answer was obviously correct. But it does not follow that the candidate was mistaken in the first place. The God of Christianity is as unique in his unity as he is in his trinity. He is the *triune* God. His oneness is unity in trinity.

In view of current heresy a few aspects of the uniqueness of the true God may well be singled out for emphasis.

Some prominent theologians who would by all means be known as Christian theologians are today rejecting the doctrine just named – that of the Trinity. More than a few spurn it as sheer speculation. At least one has asserted that as far as this doctrine is concerned, he could be rated an atheist. But the Bible, which insists that there is but one God, also distinguishes plainly between God the Father, God the Son and God the Holy Spirit as so many persons. Not only is the doctrine of the Trinity clearly implied in the baptismal formula [*Matt* 28:19] and the apostolic benediction [II *Cor* 13:14], both of which give equal honour to the Father, the Son and the Holy Spirit; the Bible states explicitly that each is God. Time and again Scripture speaks of 'God the Father'. The prologue of John's gospel is but one of the many passages that ascribe deity to Jesus. The Word that became flesh is said to be God [*John* 1:1, 14]. And in addressing Ananias the apostle Peter identified the Holy Spirit with God. Having accused Ananias of lying to the Holy Spirit, he explained, 'Thou hast not lied unto men, but unto God' [*Acts* 5:3, 4]. Not only are there so-called proof-texts for the doctrine of the Trinity; being manifest in both creation and redemption, it is woven into the very warp and woof of special revelation. God the Father created by the Word [*Gen* 1, *John* 1:3]; and the Spirit of God, moving upon the face of the waters, impregnated the earth [*Gen* 1:2]. Scripture throughout also teaches that redemption is the work of the triune God. That truth lies at the very heart of divine revelation. The Christian doctrine of the triune God and the Christian doctrine of salvation are inseparable and dependent one on the other.

It is sometimes said that Hindu theology contains an approximation to the Christian doctrine of the triune God. It speaks of Brahma the Creator, Vishnu the Preserver, and Siva the Destroyer, as together constituting Trimurti (*tri* meaning three and *murti* shape). In reality Trimurti is no approximation at all to the one God of the Bible. The Hindus have a triad of gods, which is to say that they have three gods. Nor are Brahma, Vishnu and Siva their only gods. They have gods almost innumerable besides. Hinduism is thoroughgoing pantheism and therefore polytheistic, not monotheistic, as is Christianity. If god is everything, everything is god.

Another aspect of the uniqueness of the God who has revealed himself in the Bible is his perfection. Theologians rightly ascribe various attributes to God, but it must never be forgotten that all the divine attributes are but so many manifestations of the one all-inclusive attribute of perfection. As a ray of light, when striking a prism, is broken up into the colours of the spectrum, so the light of divine perfection, when directed to human intelligence, as is done in the Bible, appears as numerous attributes. Among them are such moral attributes as goodness, holiness and justice.

Any one familiar with mythology knows that the gods and goddesses of the ancient Greeks and Romans were not always moral. It was not unusual for them to dissemble, and at times they indulged in the basest kind of moral turpitude. Aphrodite, for example, became disloyal to her husband Hephaestus and was worshipped not only as the goddess of sexual love but also as the enemy of chastity. In general, the ethnic religions are polytheistic, and a presupposition of polytheism is imperfection of one kind or another. If God is perfect, there need be no other god or gods beside him.

It goes without saying that the God of the Bible has absolute moral perfection. He is 'not a man that he should lie' [*Num* 23:19]. 'Far be it from God that he should do wickedness, and from the Almighty that he should commit iniquity' [*Job* 34:10]. Time and again he is spoken of as 'the Holy One of Israel'. In his presence the seraphs cover their faces because of his resplendent holiness and cry out to one another, 'Holy, holy, holy is the Lord of hosts' [*Isa* 6:3].

The moral perfection of the only true God shines forth brilliantly in the fact that he is at once absolute in justice and infinite in love. Both Hinduism and Buddhism speak of 'karma'. By it they mean the entire ethical consequence of one's acts fixing inescapably one's lot in the future existence. There is, then, no escape from the just penalty of sin. That is justice without mercy. On the other hand, present-day Modernism, picturing God as an over-indulgent grandfather, teaches that God, being love, overlooks and forgives sin without satisfaction. That is mercy without justice. But the God of Christianity is a God of both perfect love and perfect justice. The two meet, embrace, coalesce, at Calvary. God so loved sinners that he gave his only Son to bear the punishment of sin as their substitute. And, rather than let sin go unpunished, he exacted the utmost penalty from that substitute when, forsaking him on the accursed cross, he surrendered him to the agony of hell. When the Saviour cried out, 'My God, my God, why hast thou forsaken me?' [*Matt* 27:46] he was at the very bottom of the bottomless pit. What justice! God sent him there and he went there in order that hell-deserving sinners might go to heaven. What love! All in all, what perfection!

THE ONLY TRUE SAVIOUR

While the Bible ascribes salvation to the triune God, it usually bestows on the Son the name 'Saviour'. Before his birth the angel said to Joseph, 'Thou shalt call his name Jesus, for he will save his people from their sins' [*Matt* 1:21]. 'Jesus' means 'Saviour'.

The Bible tells us that Jesus saves completely. The Bible also tells us that only Jesus saves. Those truths stand and fall together. If Jesus did not save completely, there would be need of an associate or assistant saviour. Now that he does save completely, the sinner has no need of being saved, even in part, by Mary or any other 'saint' or himself. Jesus does all the saving. For that reason he is the one and only Saviour.

Jesus is the Christ, the Messiah, the Anointed. As such 'he is ordained of God the Father, and anointed with the Holy Spirit, to be our chief Prophet and Teacher, who has fully revealed to us the secret counsel and will of God concerning our redemption; our only High Priest, who by the one sacrifice of his body has redeemed us, and makes continual intercession for us with the Father; and our eternal King, who governs us by his Word and Spirit, and defends and preserves us in the salvation obtained for us' (Heidelberg

Catechism XII, 31). Christ saves *from* the guilt of sin, from the power of sin, from the penalty of sin, which is eternal death. He saves *for* true knowledge, perfect righteousness, complete holiness and everlasting life. Of God he is made unto us complete redemption [1 *Cor* 1:30]. In short, he is a perfect Saviour. And let it be said again, for that very reason he is the only true Saviour.

The Bible teaches most explicitly that there is no salvation outside of Jesus the Christ. He himself declared majestically, 'I am the way, the truth, and the life; no man cometh unto the Father but by me' [*John* 14:6]. Peter boldly avowed to the Jewish rulers, 'Neither is there salvation in any other; for there is none other name under heaven given among men, whereby we must be saved' [*Acts* 4:12]. Being 'able to save to the uttermost them that come unto God by him' [*Heb* 7:25], it is written of him, 'Now unto him that is able to keep you from stumbling and to set you before the presence of his glory in exceeding joy, to the only God our Saviour, through Jesus Christ our Lord, be glory, majesty, dominion and power, before all time, and now, and for evermore' [*Jude* 24, 25].

THE ONLY TRUE MORALITY

Morality is rooted in religion. That truth, although often overlooked and even denied by ignorant men, is acknowledged by all religions. However radically definitions of goodness may, and actually do, differ, there is not a religion on this globe which does not bid its adherents to be good after a fashion and to do good of a kind.

True morality is rooted in true religion. It is no accident that the 'God-is-dead theology' and the 'new morality', which in reality is immorality, are today equally popular. Ours is an age in which man is deified. If man is god, then what the great majority of men do, what 'everybody' is doing, call it lying, theft, adultery, or what you will, cannot be wrong. Some years ago I heard Stanley Jones lecture on the question 'Do Ideas Matter?' He called attention to many of the evils rampant in India and pointed out that they were directly traceable to the erroneous religious notions prevalent among the people of that land. But if the God of the Bible is the one true and living God, the keeping of his precepts is the only true morality.

What does God command? The answer can be given in one word. That word is *love*. 'Love is the fulfilling of the law' [*Rom* 13:10]. The reader is invited to a few moments of meditation on that seemingly simple, yet actually profound, truth. The surpassing excellence of Christian morality will become evident.

Why does God command love? The ultimate answer is: because he himself is love. 'God is love, and he that dwelleth in love dwelleth in God and God in him' [1 *John* 4:16]. In requiring love God requires godliness, and godliness is god-likeness. To be sure, at this point it behoves us to beware of grave misrepresentation. Man has never been God, he is not God now, and he never will be God. The difference between God and man is the difference between the infinite and the finite, and it is qualitative. Man is not even a miniature God. Yet man was created in the image and likeness of God, consisting of true knowledge of God, righteousness and holiness, and that image, lost through sin, is restored in the regenerate [*Gen* 1:26, 27; *Eph* 4:24; *Col* 3:10]. In that light the statement can stand that God requires godlikeness.

To put the same truth in a slightly different way, in requiring love God requires perfection. In the Sermon on the Mount Jesus said, 'Ye have heard that it hath been said, Thou shalt love thy neighbour and hate thine enemy. But I say unto you, Love your enemies, bless them that curse you, do good to them that hate you, and pray for them which despitefully use you and persecute you; that ye may be the children of your Father which is in heaven,' and then summarized what he had just said in the command, 'Be ye therefore perfect, even as your Father which is in heaven is perfect' [*Matt* 5:43–45, 48].

Christian morality differs radically from legalism. Legalism is obedience to the letter of the law to the neglect of the spirit; Christian morality is obedience to the spirit of the law as well as the letter. The spirit of the law is love. Strictest obedience to the law of God divorced from love for God is disobedience. Jesus had that in mind when he said, 'Except your righteousness shall exceed the righteousness of the scribes and Pharisees, ye shall in no case enter into the kingdom of heaven' [*Matt* 5:20].

Moses thus summarized the law of God: 'Hear, O Israel: the Lord our God is one Lord. And thou shalt love the Lord thy God with all thy heart, and with all thy soul, and with all thy might' [*Deut* 6:4, 5]. In answering the question which is the first commandment of all, Jesus repeated Moses's summary and added, 'The second is like, namely this, Thou shalt love thy neighbour as thyself' [*Mark* 12:28–31]. Many are of the opinion that, although natural, unregenerate man cannot keep the first of these commandments, he is able to obey the second. But that is far from true. The law of God is one. The second commandment presupposes the first and is rooted in it. Both have the same preamble: 'The Lord our God is one Lord.' The second commandment, as the first, must be obeyed for God's sake. Man must love his neighbour because he loves God. Only he who does that loves his neighbour as God requires.

Every religion has its code of ethics. So does Christianity.

The decalogue is still in force. So is the ethical teaching of the Old Testament prophets as well as that of Jesus and the apostles. The Christian code differs substantially from all other codes. But Christianity also differs radically from all other religions as to the *observance* of law. Every other religion proclaims its law and leaves it to men, depraved as they are, to obey or not to obey. Christianity not only proclaims its law but also provides for sinful men renewal of heart enabling them to obey. Every other religion is autosoteric. It tells men that they must save themselves from sin and make themselves holy. Popularly put, it commands sinners, sinking in quicksand, to lift themselves by their bootstraps. Christianity alone is heterosoteric. It proclaims Another, One who is both willing and able to rescue from sin's power and pollution and to impart holiness of heart and life. That is the Holy Spirit. He may be had for the asking [*Luke* 11:13].

All other religions tell men to be good and to do good *in order that they may be saved.* Christianity commands the Christian to be good and to do good *because he has been saved.* Significantly, God prefaced the Ten Commandments with the reminder that he was the Deliverer, the Saviour, of his people [*Exod* 20:2, *Deut* 5:6]. The Christian loves God because God first loved him and manifested that love in the gift of his only begotten Son as Saviour. Said the apostle of love, 'Herein is love, not that we loved God but that he loved us and sent his Son to be the propitiation for our sins' and, 'We love him because he first loved us' [1 *John* 4:10, 19]. It follows that Christian morality springs from saving faith in Jesus Christ, who, as gift of God's infinite love, fully satisfied the absolute justice of God by his substitutionary death on the accursed cross and by his obedience even unto death merited for hell-deserving sinners life everlasting.

XI

The antithesis of the regenerate and the unregenerate is radical

SCRIPTURE speaks of several antitheses; for example, that of Christ and Anti-Christ, that of the good angels and the fallen angels, that of believers and 'principalities, powers, the rulers of the darkness of this world, spiritual wickedness in high places' [*Eph* 6:12], that of the church and the world, that of believers and unbelievers, that of regenerate and unregenerate men. These antitheses are interrelated. In fact, they may be said to be so many facets of one grand antithesis. That truth should be borne in mind when an attempt is made to describe any one of them.

This essay will deal primarily with the antithesis of the regenerate and the unregenerate. In the light of Scripture several of its characteristics will be named.

CENTRAL IN SCRIPTURE, NOT PERIPHERAL

The Bible is the Word of God. It goes without saying that all that God says is true. It is no less obvious that all that he says is important. Yet not all things told us in the Bible are of equal importance. Some are stressed more strongly than are others. Some are supremely significant, others relatively less so. The teaching of the antithesis does not lie on the periphery of the Word of God, but is central to it. It is of the very warp and woof of Holy Writ.

At the dawn of human history God put enmity between the serpent and the woman and between their seed, and he foretold that the woman's seed would bruise the head of the serpent, whereas the serpent would bruise the heel of the woman's seed [*Gen* 3:15]. This passage is correctly denominated the *protevangelium*, the first proclamation of the gospel. Significantly, it is also the first declaration of the antithesis. At the end of time the Son of God will part men asunder even as a shepherd divides the sheep from the goats, and with the sword of his mouth he will divide the human race in two for the endless ages of eternity. Some will enter upon eternal life; others will depart into eternal punishment [*Matt* 25:31–46]. Between the aforenamed two events lies an unintermittent conflict of the woman's seed and that of the serpent. It is, indeed, *the* conflict of the ages. And it reached its climax in that event about which centres the whole of human history – the crucifixion of Jesus Christ.

Present-day denials of the antithesis are numerous. Many substitute for it the deceptive dogma of the universal fatherhood of God and the universal brotherhood of man. We are witnessing a mighty resurgence of the ancient heresy of universal salvation. Preachers and professors of theology tell us that it is inconceivable that a God of love would sentence any human being to eternal hell. Such teaching is the direct result of rejection of the Bible as the infallible Word of God.

Inexpressibly sad to say, even in relatively conservative circles there are those who belittle the antithesis. They are wont to speak of it sneeringly. For that attitude there are but two possible explanations. It is rooted either in ignorance of Holy Scripture or in a tendency to slight Scripture. It could spring from both. He who takes the Bible seriously cannot help taking the antithesis seriously. Scripture teaches it unequivocally, and Scripture's emphasis on it is truly tremendous.

A FACT, NOT A DUTY

The Bible informs us that the antithesis of the regenerate and the unregenerate is a fact. To be sure, a duty is implicit in it; but it is not itself a duty. It is an inescapable fact.

That fact is God-appointed. When our earliest ancestors had yielded to the deceiver's temptation, God did not command the woman, together with her seed, to be at enmity with Satan; he *put* enmity between them. Regeneration, by which the antithesis is brought about, is a divine work in which man is utterly passive. Nowhere does Scripture command dead sinners to bring themselves to life. 'Ye must be born again' [*John* 3:7] is an indicative, not an imperative. The apostolic exhortation, 'Awake, thou that sleepest, and arise from the dead' [*Eph* 5:14] was addressed, not to dead sinners, but to sleeping Christians who once were darkness but now were light in the Lord [v. 8]. They were commanded to arouse themselves from spiritual lethargy and to arise from among their spiritually dead pagan neighbours. Nor had they transformed themselves from darkness into light. That change was effected by God.

That the antithesis of the regenerate and the unregenerate is a God-appointed fact is the plain teaching of Scripture. Scripture is no less insistent that this fact entails a duty. The regenerate differ radically from the unregenerate. That being the case, they are in sacred duty bound to show it. The solemn admonition addressed to them, 'Walk as children of light' [*Eph* 5:8], is predicated on the fact that they are light, not darkness. God requires of his children that they manifest what they are, that they be true to their regenerate selves.

SPIRITUAL, NOT SPATIAL

That the contrast of the regenerate and the unregenerate is spiritual is self-evident. On the one hand are those who are spiritually alive, on the other hand those who are spiritually dead [*Eph* 2:1].

Strange, and also exceedingly sad, to say, throughout history God's people have times without number committed the fallacy of externalizing the antithesis. They have regarded it as spatial rather than spiritual.

No doubt the most heinous sin of ancient Israel was idolatry, worship of the false gods of the neighbouring peoples. It constituted a brazen denial of the antithesis. Another of its sins, hardly less heinous, was formalism. God complained, 'This people draw near me with their mouth, and with their lips do honour me, but have removed their heart far from me' [*Isa* 29:13]. And by the voice of his prophet God uttered the scathing denunciation, 'To what purpose is the multitude of your sacrifices unto me? . . . I am full of the burnt offerings of rams, and the fat of fed beasts; and I delight not in the blood of bullocks, or of lambs, or of he goats. When ye come to appear before me, who hath required this at your hand, to tread my courts? Bring no more vain oblations; incense is an abomination unto me' [*Isa* 1:11–13]. Formalism externalizes the antithesis. And to externalize the spiritual is to deny it.

The Pharisees of Jesus' day perverted the antithesis by making it spatial. The hermits and stylites of early Christianity tended to do likewise. So did the monks and nuns of the Middle Ages. So did the extreme Anabaptists of the Reformation age. So do the Amish of today. And so do all who deem world flight to be the essence of Christian living.

True, the antithesis has spatial implications. Christian parents will instruct their children to shun evil companions.

In the line of duty adult Christians are bound to face many temptations, but to expose oneself needlessly to temptation is to tempt God. Matrimony has a spatial as well as a spiritual aspect, and Scripture forbids the marriage of a believer to an unbeliever. No Christian may hold membership in an organization which by its constitution and persistent practices defies the law of God and in which he is forbidden to witness to the lordship of Christ. The Psalmist pronounced blessed 'the man that walketh not in the counsel of the ungodly, nor standeth in the way of sinners, nor sitteth in the seat of the scornful' [*Ps* 1:1].

However, the Saviour prayed for his own, not that they would be taken out of the world, but that they would be kept from the evil one [*John* 17:15]; and the apostle Paul advised the saints in Corinth not to break off all association with the fornicators, the covetous, the extortioners, and the idolaters of the world, for in that case they would have to go out of the world [1 *Cor* 5:9, 10].

He who externalizes the antithesis is sure to fall into a heinous sin of omission. Without contact with the world one cannot perform his duty as the salt of the earth and the light of the world [*Matt* 5:13, 14]. He is also in imminent peril of yielding to a no less heinous sin of commission. Losing sight of the spiritual character of the antithesis can hardly result in anything but unspiritual living. It is not unusual for a recluse to become a profligate. The externalization of the antithesis is a mark of sanctimony, not of sanctity.

ABSOLUTE, NOT RELATIVE

The antithesis under discussion has been described as *radical.* The difference between the regenerate and the unregenerate is not something shallow or superficial. Contrariwise, it concerns that which is deepest in man, his inmost being, the basic disposition of his soul – what the Bible calls his *heart*. In regeneration the sinner receives a new heart. The unregenerate have 'hearts of stone', the regenerate 'hearts of flesh' [*Ezek* 36:26].

Prominent theologians have not hesitated to describe the antithesis as *absolute*. That is strong language; in the estimation of some, too strong. It has been argued that the contrast between the regenerate and the unregenerate is less than absolute because they have certain things in common; for instance, the quality of humanness. That they have humanness in common cannot be denied. Man alone of all earthly creatures was made in the image of God. That image constitutes him a human being. Now, in the fall it was not entirely lost. Vestiges of it remain in the most perverse of men. However, the absolute character of the antithesis is not thus ruled out. If the regenerate and the unregenerate had nothing whatever in common, they would not even be comparable; and it hardly makes sense to speak of the antithesis of incomparables. Even Christ and Antichrist have something in common. Beyond all reasonable doubt, *the* Antichrist, who is to appear toward the end of time, will be a human person. Scripture speaks of him as 'that man of sin' and 'the son of perdition' [II *Thess* 2:3]. Christ, too, even the ascended Christ, has a human nature. Christ and Antichrist, then, have humanness in common. But who will deny that the antithesis of the two is absolute? Nor may it be overlooked that the difference between the image of God as it remains in all men and the image of God as it is restored in the regenerate is not merely quantitative but decidedly qualitative.

After all, the antithesis of the regenerate and the unregenerate is that of life and death. To be sure, it is not the antithesis of physical life and physical death. All men, with such rare exceptions as Enoch and Elijah and the less rare exception of those who remain alive at Christ's second coming, must experience the separation of body and soul. Nor is it for the present the antithesis of eternal life and eternal death. The regenerate do indeed possess eternal life even now, but the unregenerate will not be swallowed up by eternal death until the day of judgment, and in the meantime the living unregenerate may yet by the grace of God be born again. But the antithesis is that of spiritual life and spiritual death. The unregenerate is not as sound as Pelagianism asserts him to be. He is not somewhat ill, as Semi-Pelagianism teaches. Nor yet is he sick well-nigh unto death, as Arminianism would have us believe. He is 'dead' [*Eph* 2:1]. That is the essence of the scriptural doctrine of total depravity. And the regenerate is 'alive' [*Eph* 2:1]. Certainly, there are degrees of sanctification, and no saint is fully sanctified in this life. It may even be granted that the term *regeneration* can be used in the broad sense of sanctification. Then there are degrees of regeneration. But there are no degrees of regeneration in the sense of the instantaneous working of the Holy Spirit by which he makes the heretofore dead sinner alive. One is either dead or alive. There is no intermediate condition, no middle ground. It follows that the antithesis is truly absolute.

PERVASIVE, NOT PARTIAL

'Be ye not unequally yoked together with unbelievers: for what fellowship hath righteousness with unrighteousness? and what communion hath light with darkness? and what concord hath Christ with Belial? or what portion hath he that believeth with an infidel? and what agreement hath the temple of God with idols? For ye are the temple of the living God; as God hath said, I will dwell in them, and walk in them; and I will be their God, and they shall be my people. Wherefore come out from among them, and be ye separate, saith the Lord; and touch not the unclean thing; and I will receive you, and will be a Father unto you, and ye shall be my sons and daughters, saith the Lord Almighty' [II *Cor* 6:14–18].

Obviously, those verses of Scripture have a most direct bearing on the antithesis. But they are often misunderstood. They are said to condemn mixed marriages. Yet there is no such reference in the context. At most the condemnation of mixed marriages is implicit in this passage. It is said to rule out practically all association of believers with unbelievers. But that would amount to a contradiction of I *Corinthians* 5:9, 10. It is said to forbid believers to hold membership in the same organization with unbelievers. But Abraham, the father of believers, entered into a defensive league with Aner, Eshcol and Mamre, heathen Palestinian chieftains; and Scripture does not breathe an inkling of disapproval of that alliance. The meaning of II *Corinthians* 6:14–18 is most specific. There were in the church at Corinth those who had not broken completely with paganism. In uncompromising language Paul enjoined these to practise complete separation from pagan worship.

Christianity is the one and only true religion. All other religions, regardless of elements of truth contained in them, are false. Exclusiveness is of the essence of Christianity. The God of the Bible is God alone [*Ps* 86:10]. All other gods are idols. And the Christ of Scripture is the only Saviour. No man can come to the Father but by him [*John* 14:6], and his name is the only one under heaven given among men by which they must be saved [*Acts* 4:12]. Therefore Christians are unqualifiedly forbidden to participate in the worship of another religion, whether paganism, Mohammedanism, Judaism or Modernism.

Room is left for numerous contacts of the regenerate with

the unregenerate, for various associations, and for much co-operation.

Does it follow that there are areas in the lives of the regenerate and the unregenerate in which the antithesis does not come to expression? That question is as important as it is pertinent. And the answer to it is an emphatic *No.* According to Scripture the antithesis is pervasive.

Two men – one regenerate, the other unregenerate – sit at one board. They eat of the same food and drink of the same beverage. Are they doing identical things? God forbid! In principle the former does his eating and drinking, as, indeed, all that he does, to the glory of God [1 *Cor* 10:31]. The latter does nothing of the kind.

The same two men attend one church. They sit in the same pew. They sing the same songs. They contribute the same offering. They listen to the same sermon. Are they doing the same thing? Far from it. The regenerate person is worshipping God, however imperfectly. The other is merely going through the form of worship.

The same two men are members of one political party and on election day they cast their ballots for the same candidates. Is the antithesis out of the picture? Not at all. One is motivated by the fear of God, the other is not.

The same two men perform seemingly identical works of charity. Is the antithesis inoperative? No verily. The unregenerate person may well be doing that which the Word of God calls 'good'. It is altogether possible that he is manifesting 'love' for his neighbour. Did not Jesus teach that even sinners love those that love them and do good to those that do good to them [*Luke* 6:32, 33]? But he is doing only what has come to be denominated *civic* good. He is incapable of performing *spiritual* good, which the Heidelberg Catechism aptly defines as works 'which are done from true faith, according to the law of God and to his glory' [XXXIII, 91]. He is not motivated by love for God. And because his love for his neighbour does not spring from love for God it does not meet the demand of God's law. The regenerate person, on the other hand, is prompted by faith in God and love for God. In consequence he performs spiritual good. It differs qualitatively from the good done by his unregenerate fellow.

The same two men sin, for 'there is no man that sinneth not' [I *Kings* 8:46] and the best of God's children offend in many ways [*Jas* 3:2]. Surely, at this point the antithesis would seem to be inactive. The truth of the matter is that even here it asserts itself vigorously. Whatever sin he may commit, the regenerate person always sins against his will.* He, and he alone, can say with Paul, 'The good that I would I do not: but the evil which I would not, that I do. Now if I do that I would not, it is no more I that do it, but sin which dwelleth in me' [*Rom* 7:19, 20]. Even the sinning of the regenerate man differs essentially from that of the unregenerate man.

How can the antithesis help being pervasive? As has been said, it is radical. It is a matter of the *heart*. The unregenerate are controlled in all that they do by 'hearts of stone'. The regenerate are dominated in all that they do by 'hearts of flesh'. And from the heart are 'the issues of life' [*Prov* 4:23]. A man's heart is what he is. And as a man is, so he thinks and feels and wills. What he is affects every function of his soul. 'If any man be in Christ, he is a new creature: old things are passed away; behold, all things are become new' [II *Cor* 5:17]. Meyer comments, '*The old*, the pre-Christian nature and life, the pre-Christian spiritual constitution of man, *is passed away*; *behold the whole* – the whole state of man's personal life – *has become new*.'

* This statement of the author should be interpreted in terms of the text quoted thereafter (Rom. 7:19,20). Responsible action cannot be dissociated from the will. But when the believer sins, this will to sin violates what is his deepest will, namely the will to holiness. (Publisher)

ACTIVE, NOT PASSIVE

An antithesis may be passive. The peaceful co-existence of white and black is altogether possible. But such is not the antithesis under consideration. It resembles the antithesis of light and darkness. They are at odds with each other. Darkness would drive out light; light would dispel darkness. Scripture tells us that the regenerate and the unregenerate are at 'enmity' with each other [*Gen* 3:15]. In short, this antithesis is active.

That the unregenerate are active in their opposition to the regenerate is a frequent and emphatic teaching of Holy Writ. Throughout history the serpent and his seed have been bruising the heel of the woman's seed. Cain killed Abel. The Egyptians cruelly oppressed God's covenant people. The heathen nations were bent on destroying Israel. That activity reached its climax when the world, a worldly church included, crucified the Christ. But the world's hatred was not burned out on that occasion. Christ's disciples have experienced it throughout the ages. Said Jesus, 'If ye were of the world, the world would love his own: but because ye are not of the world, but I have chosen you out of the world, therefore the world hateth you. Remember the word that I said unto you, The servant is not greater than his lord. If they have persecuted me, they will also persecute you' [*John* 15:19, 20].

The attitude of the regenerate to the unregenerate is quite different from that of the unregenerate to the regenerate. The unregenerate hate the regenerate; the regenerate love the unregenerate. The difference is a striking manifestation of the antithesis. As God loves his enemies, so God's children love their enemies, albeit imperfectly [*Matt* 5:43–48]. They pray for their persecutors as Jesus prayed for those who were nailing him to the cross [*Luke* 23:34] and as Stephen prayed for those who were stoning him to death [*Acts* 7:60]. And by proclaiming to them the gospel of the grace of God they seek to persuade them to believe on the Saviour. In Christ's stead they pray them to be reconciled to God [II *Cor* 5:20].

That is not the entire picture. The regenerate also oppose the unregenerate. They condemn their evil works. They denounce their proud works. They would thwart their wicked designs. And, paradoxical as it may be, when the unregenerate blatantly defy the Most High and brazenly give vent to their hatred of him, the regenerate are constrained by their very love for God to exclaim, 'Do not I hate them, O God, that hate thee? and am I not grieved with those that rise up against thee? I hate them with a perfect hatred: I count them mine enemies' [*Ps* 139:21, 22]. And that note is heard not merely in a few so-called imprecatory Psalms, but it sounds forth clearly throughout the Book of Psalms, in the woes pronounced by the Son of God, in the anathemas of inspired Paul, and in the loud cry of 'the souls of them that were slain for the word of God and for the testimony which they held', issuing from under the altar in heaven: 'How long, O Lord, holy and true, dost thou not judge and avenge our blood on them that dwell on the earth?' [*Rev* 6:9, 10].

ISSUING IN CONQUEST, NOT FLIGHT

The antithesis is spiritual, not spatial. For that reason world flight must be condemned. There is another reason. The antithesis must issue, and will, in conquest of the world, and flight can hardly result in conquest.

Two stories from Greek mythology illustrate rather well the difference between world flight and world conquest. A certain island was inhabited by Sirens, creatures that were half woman and half bird. So alluring was their song that any mariners who came within hearing distance were irresistibly drawn to the island. But no sooner did they set foot on shore than the Sirens would tear them in pieces and devour them. Odysseus's ship was about to enter the danger zone. Aware of the peril besetting him and his crew, he stopped their ears with wax and had them bind him firmly to the mast with strict orders to pay no heed to his pleading for release. Those measures resembled world flight. Orpheus and his Argonauts, too, neared the island of the Sirens, and he also was aware of imminent peril. But he took an altogether different measure to insure the safety of his men and himself. Playing on his lyre, he made music of such superior charm that none gave the slightest heed to the song of the Sirens. That resembled world conquest.

Let not God's people think that they have discharged their duty when they have stopped their ears to the temptations of the world. What they must do is to drown out the voice of the tempter by singing the songs of Zion. In other words, they must crowd out evil from their lives by the doing of good. And, to go far beyond our illustration, they must declare the gospel of the grace of God to the four corners of the earth in order that sinners from every kindred and tongue and people and nation may be won for Christ and brought into the fold of his church. That is a most important aspect of world conquest. Yet it is not the whole of it.

The apostle John said, 'This is the victory that overcometh the world, even our faith' [1 *John* 5:4]. The eleventh chapter of Hebrews presents a long list of such as overcame the world by faith. Those overcame who through faith subdued kingdoms, wrought righteousness, obtained promises, stopped the mouths of lions, quenched the violence of fire, escaped the edge of the sword, waxed valiant in fight, turned to flight the armies of aliens [vv. 33, 34]. But unbelievable though it may seem, they also overcame who were tortured, not accepting deliverance, had trial of cruel mockings and scourgings, yes, of bonds and imprisonment, were stoned, were sawn asunder, were slain with the sword, and wandered in deserts and in mountains, in dens and caves of the earth [vv. 35–38]. For in all these things they were more than conquerors through him that loved them [*Rom* 8:37].

An amazing teaching of Scripture is that believers are owners of all things. Paul wrote to the Christians in wealthy Corinth, 'Whether Paul, or Apollos, or Cephas, or the world, or life, or death, or things present, or things to come: all are yours' [1 *Cor* 3:22]. In 'all', the products of the common grace of God are included; for example, Greek art, Roman law, the learning of the ancient world, English literature, modern science. To be sure, believers are warned not to use the world to the full because its fashion passes away [1 *Cor* 7:31]. Yet it belongs to the regenerate in a sense in which it does not belong to the unregenerate. This is their Father's world and therefore theirs. They are to use radio, television, aeronautics, atomic energy, and countless other things to the glory of God and his Christ. That, too, is a phase of world conquest.

God gave Christ to the church that he might be head over the church, to be sure, but also over all things [*Eph* 1:22]. The kingship of Christ over all things must be proclaimed by the church. It must demand of men everywhere that they acknowledge Christ as king over every domain of life. The regenerate must declare a Christian view of the whole of life and all of the world. They must insist on Christian education, Christian science, Christian art, Christian culture, Christian relations between labour and industry, Christian politics, Christian internationalism, a Christian society as well as a Christian church.

The antithesis of the regenerate & the unregenerate is radical

And whether today and tomorrow men hear or forbear, one day all things will be subdued unto the Christ [1 *Cor* 15:27]; at the name of Jesus every knee will bow, of things in heaven, and things in earth, and things under the earth; and every tongue will confess that Jesus Christ is Lord [*Phil* 2:10, 11]; great voices in heaven will sing, 'The kingdoms of this world are become the kingdoms of our Lord, and of his Christ; and he shall reign for ever and ever' [*Rev* 11:15].

XII

Christianity is history, doctrine, conduct

CHRISTIANITY has fallen on evil days. So evil are these days that many describe them as the post-Christian era. Christianity is said to be a passé religion.

According to the Bible Christianity is a matter of history, a matter of doctrine, and a matter of conduct. All three of these aspects of Christianity are being rejected by a large and influential segment of what is commonly called Christendom. Historic Christianity, based as it is on the Bible, is being denied openly, even vigorously, by those of its own household.

Deeply grieved though they are, believers are not discouraged. In spite of heresy and persecution Christianity has survived for some twenty centuries. As for the future, Christ's promise is sure that the gates of hell will prevail neither against Christian truth nor against the church professing that truth [*Matt* 16:16–18]. 'All flesh is as grass and all the glory of man as the flower of grass. The grass withereth and the flower thereof falleth away; but the word of the Lord endureth for ever' [1 *Pet* 1:24, 25]. Said Jesus, 'Heaven and earth shall pass away; but my words shall not pass away' [*Luke* 21:33].

CHRISTIANITY IS HISTORY

A large part of the Bible is history. Of the thirty-nine books of the Old Testament the first seventeen and of the twenty-seven books of the New Testament the first five are usually classified as historical books. Nor is history confined to these books. The Christian religion is based upon the historical events related in the Bible.

Throughout the history of Christianity Bible history has been under fire. Docetism, a heresy almost as old as Christianity itself, merged the truth and reality of Christ's human nature in a mere phantom. In the nineteenth century more than one European scholar denied Jesus as a historical person. More recently the dialectical theology has relegated much of Bible history to the realm of the supra-historical. Karl Barth distinguishes between *Geschichte* and *Historie*, which means that somehow he does not regard such events as the virgin birth and the bodily resurrection of Jesus as history in the same sense in which it is history that Napoleon Bonaparte was defeated by Wellington and Blücher in the Battle of Waterloo on the 18th of June, 1815, and that Abraham Lincoln was shot in Ford's theatre by John Wilkes Booth on April 14, 1865. Rudolph Bultmann is bold to say that much of Bible history is pure myth, teaching important truths, to be sure, but never having transpired.

Why is it that much of Bible history has been assailed in the past and is being assailed today? One reason, and a very significant one, is that many object to the supernatural. Miracles abound in Bible history, but of the miraculous many will have nothing. However, to strip Christianity of the supernatural is to destroy Christianity.

It is not at all difficult to single out events in Bible history with which Christianity stands or falls.

The account of creation given in the early chapters of Genesis is history. If God did not create the universe, then what becomes of the Christian teaching of divine transcendence, that is to say, that God exists before and above the universe? And if God did not create the universe, how did the universe come into being? Did it just happen or is matter eternal? In either case the universe is independent of God. In the latter case is it not reasonable to suppose that the universe itself is God?

The account in the third chapter of Genesis of the fall of man into sin is history. The apostle Paul placed the disobedience of Adam in the identical category of complete actuality when he wrote, 'As by one man's disobedience many were made sinners, so by the obedience of one shall many be made righteous' [*Rom* 5:19]. To deny the historicity of the disobedience of the first Adam is to cancel out the historicity of the obedience of the last Adam. But if the perfect obedience of Christ is eliminated, what remains of the Christian doctrine of salvation?

God prefaced the decalogue with the declaration, 'I am the Lord thy God, which have brought thee out of the land of Egypt, out of the house of bondage' [*Ex* 20:2, *Deut* 5:6]. It was a reminder of history. The inescapable implication was that as Israel's Saviour God had the right to lay down the law for his people and to expect his people to obey. Does it not follow that he who denies such miraculous events as the ten plagues visited upon the Egyptians and the crossing of the Red Sea on dry ground by the Israelites is tampering with the cogency and compulsion of God's law?

When the angel Gabriel announced to Mary of Nazareth that she would give birth to a son who would be both Saviour and King, she queried, 'How shall this be, seeing I know not a man?' The angel answered, 'The Holy Ghost shall come upon thee, and the power of the Highest shall overshadow thee: therefore also that holy thing which shall be born of thee shall be called the Son of God' [*Luke* 1:31–35]. The conclusion is inescapable that if Jesus was not conceived by the

Holy Spirit and born of the virgin Mary, but was born of Mary by Joseph or some other man, he had no right to be called the Son of God. How clear that the historical event of the virgin birth is of the essence of Christianity!

The same holds obviously of the bodily resurrection of Jesus. In the fifteenth chapter of his first epistle to the Corinthians Paul dealt with the bodily resurrection of Christ and his own. Of the resurrection of Christ's body in the most literal and actual sense he said, 'If Christ be not risen, then is our preaching vain, and your faith is vain. . . . And if Christ be not raised, your faith is vain; ye are yet in your sins. Then they also which are fallen asleep in Christ are perished. If in this life only we have hope of Christ, we are of all men most miserable' [1 *Cor* 15:14–19].

CHRISTIANITY IS DOCTRINE

Christian doctrine has always been under fire. Today it is under extremely heavy fire from many directions.

For decades liberal theologians have been dinning into our ears the vapid maxim, 'Christianity is not a doctrine but a life.' Sad to say, non-confessional churches and missions keep repeating the slogan, 'No creed but Christ.' Exceedingly sad to say, in many confessional churches there is a strong trend toward scrapping the historic creeds of Christendom or at best assigning them to a museum of antiquities. Within Christendom there is a strong demand for an undogmatic Christianity. Many avowed preachers of Christianity stress subjective religious experience at the expense of objective Christian doctrine.

It would be a simple matter to draw up a long list of doctrines all of which are essential to Christianity. To enumerate a few, there is the doctrine of the Holy Trinity, which is to say that there is but one God and that in the godhead there are three persons – the Father, the Son and the Holy Spirit; the doctrine of the sovereignty of God, which is to say that God is not dependent on any of his creatures and that man is responsible to God for all he does or leaves undone; the doctrine of the person of Jesus Christ, which is to say that he is one divine person with both a divine and a human nature; the doctrine of the sinlessness of Jesus Christ, which is to say that only if he had no sin of his own could he atone for the sin of others; the doctrine of the depravity of man, which is to say that, being spiritually dead, he is utterly dependent on the grace of God for salvation; the doctrine of the substitutionary atonement, which is to say that Christ's death on the cross, instead of making it possible for sinners to save themselves, actually saves sinners; the doctrine of the new birth, which is to say that the Holy Spirit, without any co-operation on the part of the sinner, can and does in the twinkling of an eye, make dead sinners alive; the doctrine of justification by faith only, which is to say that the sinner is acquitted at the judgment seat of God and given the title to eternal life, not on account of his works but only because of the merits of Christ through the instrumentality of a living and active faith; the doctrine of Christ's second coming, which is to say that he is going to return to earth to raise the dead, judge the world, and take his own unto himself in eternal glory; and that doctrine which constitutes the very heart of the Bible, salvation by grace, which is to say that salvation is a hundred per cent of the triune God, even faith being a gift of God.

He who attempts to stress Christian living by disparaging Christian doctrine is guilty of a most serious blunder. He neglects the important fact that Christian living is rooted in Christian doctrine. It follows that he is undermining both Christian conduct and Christian truth, one as much as the other.

OTHER BOOKS PUBLISHED BY THE BANNER OF TRUTH TRUST

THE GLORIOUS BODY OF CHRIST

R. B. Kuiper

'Glorious' is probably the last adjective most modern writers would use to describe the Christian Church. Yet R. B. Kuiper chose his title, 'The Glorious Body of Christ', advisedly, for he wished to emphasize what he believed to be a sadly neglected aspect of the subject, that the Church of Christ is glorious.

Dr Kuiper, who died in 1966, was for many decades a teacher of theology, and his great concern was for the popular presentation of Christian doctrine. His own books went far to meet that need, notably *God-Centred Evangelism, For Whom Did Christ Die?* and the above title.

In addition to his vigorous and clear style, Kuiper is also noted for the comprehensive way in which he treats his subject. 'The Glorious Body' contains no less than fifty-three chapters, and among the aspects of the subject dealt with are unity, the marks of the Church, the offices of the Church, its responsibilities and privileges, and the Church and the world.

Although this book is worthy of the widest possible circulation, it may be particularly commended as a manual for office-bearers in the Church.

392 *pages*, 21s

*GOD-CENTRED EVANGELISM

R. B. Kuiper

R. B. Kuiper here presents the theology of evangelism in a logical and concise manner. This is one of the most comprehensive and helpful works on all aspects of evangelism.

The book begins with God as the Author of evangelism, and shows the relation of his Love, Election, Covenant and Commission to it. There are chapters on the Scope, Urgency, Motive, Aim, Agent, Approach, Means, Message, Method, Effectiveness and Triumph of Evangelism. Dr Kuiper also deals with Zeal for, Co-operation in, and Resistance to Evangelism.

240 *pages, paperback,* 6s

*Not available to the USA or Canada

THE FORGOTTEN SPURGEON

Iain Murray

Wilbur Smith wrote concerning Spurgeon in 1955: 'I have come to the strong conviction that the Christian church today has not yet seen a fully adequate, definitive life of this mighty preacher of the grace of God'. This new book on Spurgeon does not aim to supply that need, for it is not a biography; but it does throw light on the cause of the deficiency and on the reasons which have given rise to the superficial image of him as a genial Victorian pulpiteer, a kind of grandfather of modern evangelicalism.

Iain Murray traces the main lines of Spurgeon's spiritual thought in connection with the three great controversies in his ministry – the first was his stand against the diluted Gospel fashionable in the London to which the young preacher came in the 1850's; the second, the famous 'Baptismal Regeneration' debate of 1864 (a debate which placed the same strain on evangelical unity as the ecumenical movement is doing today); lastly, the lacerating Down-Grade controversy of 1887–1892 when Spurgeon sought to awaken Christians to the danger of the Church 'being buried beneath the boiling mud-showers of modern heresy'.

224 *pages, paperback,* 5s

WARNINGS TO THE CHURCHES

J. C. Ryle

Some of Ryle's most pungent writings have hitherto tended to be lost in his larger volumes. This book brings together eight addresses with a common theme. Together they sound a prophetic and much needed warning to the churches.

'I fear much for many professing Christians. I see no sign of fighting in them, much less of victory. They never strike one stroke on the side of Christ. They are at peace with His enemies. They have no quarrel with sin. – I warn you, this is not Christianity. This is not the way to heaven.

'I often fear much for those who hear the Gospel regularly. I fear lest you become so familiar with the sound of its doctrines, that insensibly you become dead to its power. I fear lest your religion should sink down into vague talk about your own weakness and corruption, and a few sentimental expressions about Christ, while real, practical fighting on Christ's side is altogether neglected. Oh! beware of this state of mind.'

176 *pages, paperback,* 5s

FOR A TESTIMONY

Bruce Hunt

Bruce Hunt, an American Presbyterian missionary working among Koreans, narrates his experiences in Manchuria during the Second World War, when he was imprisoned by the invading Japanese. Maltreated, half-starved, tormented, released, re-arrested, cast greatly upon God he was brought through to the praise of divine grace. But what inspires the reader is the author's burden for the Korean Christians, who loved not their lives unto death. The account of their consistency under persecution is a great encouragement to missionary endeavour.

The late Edward J. Young of Westminster wrote: 'The Rev. Bruce F. Hunt is a highly respected missionary of the Orthodox Presbyterian Church. Born in Korea, he has spent practically his entire life in that country preaching the unsearchable riches of Jesus Christ. His devoted labours have been deeply blessed of God. In the present book his love to Christ shines forth on every page. This is not an ordinary book but here is the fascinating account of one who, even in severe trial, was faithful to his Lord. It is a book that all Christians should read, and if non-Christians would read it, they might come to understand the secret of such a life.'

160 *pages, illus, paperback,* 5*s*

THE MYSTERY OF PROVIDENCE

John Flavel

Do we believe that everything in the world and in our own lives down to the minutest details is ordered by the providence of God? Do we ever take time to observe and meditate on the workings of providence? If not, are we missing much?

It should be a delight and pleasure to us to discern how God works all things in the world for His own glory and His people's good. But it should be an even greater pleasure to observe the particular designs of providence in our own lives. 'O what a world of rarities,' says John Flavel, 'are to be found in providence . . . With what profound wisdom, infinite tenderness and incessant vigilance it has managed all that concerns us from first to last.' It was to persuade Christians of the excellency of observing and meditating upon this that Flavel first published his *Mystery of Providence* in 1678. Since then the work has gone through many editions.

Based on the words 'God that performeth all things for me' [Ps. 57 . 2] this work shows us how providence works for us in every stage and experience of our lives. The book is richly illustrated from the lives of believers and from the author's wide reading in church history. There are avenues of spiritual knowledge and experience opened to the Christian in this work which he probably never knew existed.

224 pages, paperback, 4s 6d

THE BANNER OF TRUTH MAGAZINE

Editor: Iain Murray

The magazine, commenced in 1955, paved the way for the republication programme of the Trust and its readers have played a major part in making that programme possible. Following a re-examination of what the role of the magazine should be, it is now in a new format, some forty pages in length and designed as a popular counterpart to the books. Articles of both contemporary and historical nature are included, with a devotional and doctrinal emphasis.

The associate editors are John R. de Witt, Paul Helm, Donald MacLeod and Geoffrey Thomas and the business editor is John J. Murray.

Published monthly, price 1s

Subscription: one year, 15s two years, 25s